*To
Bob Schreiter,
Many thanks for
your kindness +
hospitality
Gordon May 1997*

RELIGION IN
AUSTRALIAN CULTURE

Gideon Goosen

RELIGION IN AUSTRALIAN CULTURE

An anthropological view

ST PAULS

The following permissions and sources are acknowledged:
extracts from: *Creating a Nation* by Patricia Grimshaw et al, Penguin Books Australia Ltd;
illustration by: Jon Goosen of *The Dominant and Subculture* (page 57); graphs of world religions and christian denominations by Chris O'Mahony (page 82); cartoons by: Jenny Coopes (page 61), E Emilsen from *A Whiff of Heresy* (page 66), Kerry Millard (page 70), Rocco Fazzari (page 81), from *The Rock* (page 117), from *Australians, A Historical Dictionary*, Sydney, Fairfax, Syme and Weldon, 1987, p.256 (page 126), Chris Morgan (page 167), Paul Johnson (page 170), Terry Wilcox (page 182), Paul Dallimore (page 191);
photos of: Dirimera and Konachi, from JS Battye Library, Perth, (page 98), Bishop John Cani, from the Archives of the Catholic Diocese of Rockhampton (page 128), The Blessing of the Fleet, from *The Catholic Weekly*, Sydney (page 158);
Used with permission.
Every effort has been made to obtain the necessary permissions for material used in this publication.

RELIGION IN AUSTRALIAN CULTURE:
an anthropological view
© Gideon Goosen, 1997

First published, February 1997

National Library of Australia
Cataloguing-in-Publication Data:
Gideon Goosen
Religion in Australian culture: an anthropological view
Bibliography.
Includes index
ISBN 1 875570 90 X
1. Religion and culture - Australia - History
2. Australia - Religious life and customs - History. I. Title.
306.60994
Cover design: Photographs by courtesy of National Council of Churches in Australia.

Published by
ST PAULS PUBLICATIONS - Society of St Paul
60-70 Broughton Rd - PO Box 906 - Strathfield, NSW 2135

ST PAULS PUBLICATIONS ——————————————————
is an activity of the Priests and Brothers of the Society of St Paul who proclaim the Gospel through the media of social communication.

Endorsements

Social cohesion in Australia requires that we recognise our differences and learn to negotiate them. Faith, although critical to so many Australian lives, is a largely neglected area of study. No understanding of multiculturalism in Australia would be complete without a reflection on religion. This book, with its anthropological orientation to faith, is a valuable contribution to both scholarship and public understanding of Australia's cultural diversity.

Professor Mary Kalantzis
Director, Institute of Interdisciplinary Studies
James Cook University, Queensland

I am very happy to commend this work to all students and others as a model of how to integrate into broader fields, such as religious studies, the principles underlying the benefits of our cultural and linguistic diversity.

The text does not seek to avoid the big issues raised by this approach: its objective yet robust approach challenges readers to consider how social factors give rise to concepts of one superior culture. It also examines the implications of one culture dominating others and the consequences of stereotyping ethnic communities. These are questions which are intensely relevant to our nation today, and I welcome this study which will assist people with concerns for maintaining ethical standards in our society. It will help them to articulate a compassionate and broadly humanitarian point of view.

Philip Ruddock MP
Minister for Immigration and Multicultural Affairs
Parliament House
Canberra, ACT

From the author

I wish to thank a number of people who have helped in the long process which results in a book like this. I always feel that in many ways books are a collective achievement. Ideas and how they might be linked are around us all the time and we use them not always knowing their origins. Many people who have influenced us go unacknowledged.

In many ways Fr Cyril Hally has been the inspiration behind my interest, and subsequently this book, by his lectures and writing over nearly twenty years now. Sometimes we specifically ask our colleagues for comments. This I did and would like now to acknowledge those who read one or more chapters of the book and made perceptive and constructive comments: Prof I. Breward, Mr G. English, Fr C. Hally, Dr C. Hill, Mr C. McGillion, and Dr M. Prentis.

I wish to thank also those who in conversation were able to provide me with information and insights about how religion functions in our society and especially those in the Uniting Church in Australia who gave their comments on the changes consequent to the union of 1977.

I must thank my students who over the years have taken up the challenges of the perspectives of this book and found them exciting.

Gideon Goosen
Australian Catholic University
Strathfield, NSW

To
Cyril Hally
missionary anthropologist
and
Columban priest

Contents

Illustrations, graphs, diagrams, cartoons

Introduction

The Australian parliament begins its work every day with the recital of *The Lord's Prayer*. When the new parliament buildings in Canberra were opened officially the ceremony was commenced with prayers by various religious leaders. These are clear illustrations of the existence of some kind of relationship between religion and Australian culture which confronts one at every turn in Australian life. The relationship is both historical in its origins and contemporary in its application. It is this relationship which will be explored further in this book but before that can be done, the title and the contents of what follows need some further introduction and explanation.

There is an increased interest in culture today especially in a country like Australia for many reasons. The most obvious one is the fact that Australia has become very multicultural especially in this century. Through-out the world cultures have asserted themselves progressively in the post-colonial age. In 1993 the celebration of *The Year of Indigenous Peoples* helped to highlight the existence and exploitation of many indigenous peoples. As we now try to understand some of these old cultures we begin to appreciate anew the meaning of values and culture.

Religion too has seen a revival throughout the world. The Arab-Israeli Wars, the stoic and defiant figure of Khomeini in Iran, the Gulf War of 1991, not to speak of public figures like Cat Stevens or Mike Tyson converting to Islam - all are incidents which have raised the profile of religion (and Islam in particular) throughout the world and certainly in Australia.

During the Gulf War there was an incident where sailors on an Australian naval ship dressed up like Arabs and then mimicked their prayer ritual. This was played back on some television news broadcasts and elicited strong protest from Muslim communities and others. The Australian government had to apologise for the incident; one of the effects of which was that it made ordinary Anglo-Celtic Australians realise that one could not ridicule other religions willy-nilly. It might be all right for Dave Allen to joke about the pope, but it is quite a different matter when it comes to Muslims and their religion.

Renewed interest in religion in general is manifest, too, in a certain restlessness among westerners in pursuit of something more than materialism. The New Age movement, interest in astrology, new religious movements, charismatic groups, creation spirituality[1], paganism, are all, in their own way, such manifestations of a search for something beyond the jejune.

Structured research into religion in Australia has taken on increased significance this century with the establishment of departments of religious studies in some universities and by more formalised research and professional structures such as the *Australian Christian Research Association (CRA)* and the *Australian Association for the Study of Religion (AASR)*.

The empirical side of research has picked up in recent decades and includes investigation into the correlates of religiosity with researchers like Bouma, Dixon, McAllister, Kaldor, McCallum, Blomberry and Hughes. The social context of religious bodies has been researched by Dempsey, Bodycomb, Black, Hogan, Humphrey, Millikan, O'Farrell, Lewins, and McKay. Aboriginal religion has received attention from people like Stanner, Rowley, Elkin and more recently Swain and Stockton while distinctive aspects of religion in Australia have been reflected in the work of Mol, Bouma, Breward, Glasner, Turner, Grocott, and Shaw.

There are plenty of books which deal with religion in Australia from the historical, sociological and theological viewpoints. This book does not attempt to replicate any of these, but to view religion as far as possible from the point of view of cultural anthropology. It is not a theological view of religion nor a commentary from the viewpoint of a committed believer although I am aware that my biases inevitably will show through. It is an attempt to tease out the meaning of culture and religion, to put the two concepts together in the context of the Australian scene and to see what their relationship has been and is currently. It is an attempt to throw an anthropological grid over Australian religious history past and present, and to see what insights emerge. This will be done through examples both past and present.

The purpose of doing this is to understand better the profundity of culture and how religion is part of a culture and can change. This well could lead to our all being more understanding, more tolerant of other religions and other cultural manifestations. This is particularly relevant in this age of ecumenical and interfaith dialogue. In doing so, the use of sociological insights and paradigms is at times unavoidable since the two disciplines often overlap. It also emphasises the point that no one discipline is sufficient by itself. The bibliography is eloquent evidence of this. I am indebted to historical accounts at every turn.

Australia is at the point of needing greater understanding of culture, subcultures, polyethnicity and cultural pluralism as the weight of multiculturalism begins to be felt in real, everyday ways. When a building development plan for a new mosque is introduced in local councils, when rioting between Aborigines and the police in Bourke or Wilcannia[2] becomes so bad the town's existence is threatened through mass withdrawals, or when the Hindmarsh Bridge[3] and women's business hits the headlines, it is time to ask ourselves if we understand enough about culture and cultures to cope with these incidents. At times like these the implications of multiculturalism are felt. The honeymoon period of multiculturalism in Australia is over and the more demanding period of understanding and living with a great diversity of cultures is upon us.

Chapters 1, 2 and 3 attempt to explain the main concepts in anthropology and religion that will provide the framework for the remaining chapters. It is not enough for people to remain at the level of appreciating folk dancing, national costumes or cuisines from various cultures. The time has come to get a firmer grasp of what culture is, how it originates and how it operates and changes, if the basis of a harmonious multicultural society is to be established. For these reasons it will not do to start reading this book at chapter 3 or 4. The first two chapters are essential for the success of this project. The same applies to religion. The myth that religion is totally divine and unrelated to culture has to be debunked.

Chapters 4 and 5 apply the conceptual framework and terminology outlined earlier and summarised at the end of chapter 3, to some aspects of Australian religious history. These examples are selective and limited as they are meant to be illustrative not comprehensive. That more examples tend to be from Roman Catholicism than from other denominations betrays my own enculturation but the principles can be applied to any denomination or religion.

In chapter 6 I have chosen the media as just one of many possible areas to investigate using the same framework. Theoretically any area could have been chosen - art, music, literature, or some other manifestations of the human spirit. I chose the media[4] because it is a strong manifestation of modernity and because of the role it plays in the processes of enculturation, diffusion and acculturation in our Australian culture. The methodology used in this chapter is different from chapters 4 and 5 by reason of the topic. The approach tends to be bibliographic but the anthropological concepts and terminology are still used in the same way as in the other chapters. The bigger picture of the understanding of culture as summarised at the end of chapter 3 is more implicit than explicit in this chapter.

In this book I have used the term 'Anglo-Celtic' to indicate the cultures that come from Great Britain, Northern Ireland and the Republic of Ireland. That would include the Anglo culture of England and the Celtic cultures of Wales, Scotland and Ireland. The term is not perfect as Donald Horne has vigorously indicated,[5] but I prefer it to 'British/Irish' since it is already in use and secondly, it does convey a certain meaning to me, namely the collective cultures from England, Ireland, Scotland and Wales. On occasions the term 'British Culture' seems more accurate when only the British component is intended. Let me also add a word about the name 'Roman Catholic'. Although that is the formal nomenclature and employed in World Council of Churches circles, I shall use the more familiar and simpler 'Catholic' which is common usage in Australia.

A word about the cartoons in this book: they are intended to be light-hearted but not frivolous. They bear a serious side to them once the laughter has settled.

The intended readers of this book are all those who wish to see the religion/culture relationship from a new perspective. They could be those well-read in theology or those with little or no formal knowledge of religious or cultural studies. Indeed those from the former group may well have the greater difficulty with a new perspective on religion.

I am sure my biases run through this book as with any author. What is important is not that readers agree with me but that what is presented stimulates reflection. In the section entitled *Points to ponder* at the end of each chapter, the questions are intended to assist further this reflection and/or discussion.

1

What is culture?

The word culture is used in many different ways. People speak about pop culture or pop music, they speak about Australia being a multicultural country, and about the need for cross-cultural studies. The popular comedy play, *Wog-a-rama* deals with different cultural groups and their customs. Someone who is being boorish is said to have no culture while the Aborigines are said to be in danger of losing their culture. Former polytechnics or colleges of advanced education that have become universities are said to have had to change their culture. To observe the Grand Final of Netball, Rugby League or Australian Rules, is to see the netball or football culture in action. At institutions of learning 'Cultural Studies ', a very broad concept, is now the in-thing.

But what does it all mean? What is the meaning of the word 'culture' which is used in so many apparently different ways? I hope to clarify the idea of culture and at least some of its meanings as we go along.

What is anthropology?

It will come as no surprise to say that there are many definitions of culture. The approach that I will take will be from the point of view of cultural anthropologists because it is an approach to culture that has not been widely used by the general public but offers new and helpful insights both into culture in general and into how religion operates.

Broadly speaking, anthropology (the study of human beings) is divided into two main branches, physical and cultural anthropology. Physical anthropology investigates the biological aspects of human beings and need not concern us here. Cultural anthropology, on the other hand, does concern us directly. It describes the forms of social organisation and the cultural systems of human groups. It includes the subdivisions of archaeology, linguistic anthropology and ethnology.

Ethnology analyses and compares the way of life of peoples, both living and dead, in historical perspective. It uses in its study the individual, particular studies called ethnographic studies, done by fieldworkers. It is important to note that cultural anthropology is concerned not only with study of primal groups although this is where it started in the nineteenth century. If that were the case, then cultural anthropology would cease once the last primal societies had disappeared. It is very much concerned with contemporary societies as well.

The science of cultural anthropology is fairly new as a discipline in historical terms. It goes back to the nineteenth century to people like Murdock, Kroeber, Bachofen, Maine, de Coulange, McLennan, Tylor, Lubbock, Morgan and Spencer. In their observations of human societies, they were fascinated by the different lifestyles of people, and with great difficulty tried to explain what they observed with various theories.

Human nature and universals: what are they?

Before we look at theories, I want to raise the concepts of human nature and universals (a pattern that is basic to human nature and common to all societies). What is human nature? Is there a common humanity? If so do universals exist? Can they be listed? These two concepts are important, as we shall see, in terms of the theories of culture that follow. As we will see, while there is agreement on a common humanity, there is no unanimity on the issue of universals.

Human nature is difficult to define. Rationality is one dimension of human nature and so important that Aristotle defined human beings as 'rational animals'. We speak about human actions as the actions of people as opposed to animals. This implies an intellect, virtues, feelings, sense appetites, will, the freedom to choose certain actions over others and that inestimable quality, risibility. From this perspective, then, human nature covers a range of human possibilities. It is the human capacity for, or tendency towards these actions which provides a common base for all societies.

Human nature or this common humanity has been envisaged in different ways at different times. Geertz makes the point about the Enlightenment having a very rosy and a very uniformitarian idea of what human nature was.[6] Humankind lived in harmony with nature, well-organised and invariant in its uniformity. Humankind paralleled the Newtonian system of the natural sciences and the universe where everything was identified, put in its place and ran according to well-defined rules. Thus as regards humankind and human nature all was clear and simple. The vast differences in customs, beliefs, practices, rituals viewed diachronically and synchronically counted as nothing in determining human nature which underpinned it all. (This fitted in well with the theological approach to monogenism and explains part of the quasi-rejection of polygenism by the Catholic magisterium for one.[7])

With the rise of anthropological fieldwork, formal and informal, this simple view came to be challenged with the pendulum swinging to the current state of affairs where understandings about human beings, human nature and universals are unclear and complex. In the wake of all the fieldwork, many theories of anthropology saw the light of day. In time these theories evoked parallel theories in other disciplines, e.g., theology re-examined the nature of humankind. In this century Karl Rahner, Karl Barth, Paul Tillich, Edward Schillebeeckx, Bernard Lonergan and others, have developed new Christian anthropologies which underpin their new theologies.

Some anthropologists attempted to go behind the practices they observed and asked the question whether there was some substratum called human and whether there was a common cultural pattern. Redfield writing in 1925, in his Introduction to Malinowski's book, *Magic, Science and Religion and Other Essays*, refers to 'a common human nature and a universal cultural pattern'. Surely, the argument went, there are some things that all humankind will agree upon, such as notions of right or wrong, beauty, reality - a sort of common denominator of culture (a *consensus gentium*, the consensus of all humankind). Others came to the position that there was no such substratum or consensus. These two groups aligned themselves either on the side of evolution or relativism.

Other disciplines have different ideas on the *humanum*. The philosopher, Kant, held that human beings have transcendental knowledge, for example, the innate ability to recognise the concept that two and two are four. The theologian Rahner speaks of human beings as having a transcendental opening to the infinite. Biblical scholars might prefer to identify the human by describing how it manifests itself: to be human is to love, die, marry, have children, belong to a family, grow personally, celebrate, succeed, fail, forgive - in short, the recurrent themes in which the biblical narratives revel. These for some would be all examples of universals springing from a common *humanum*. How-ever it is not that easy. One must be careful to distinguish between the human need to love and the cultural expression thereof in terms of wife, family, friends. One must distinguish between the need for sexual expression as part of human nature and the cultural expression thereof in terms of marriage and incest taboos which might or might not be universal.

If one's position is that of an evolutionist then there are universals that all human beings will have. Not all anthropologists use it in this sense. Some restrict it to one society or to western societies. In the words of one author: 'Norms that apply to every member of a society, such as the use of the fork in western societies are called universals'.[8] Luzbetak uses 'universal' in this restricted sense: 'Some patterns are expected of every normal member of society, for example, the vernacular language. Such patterns are known as "universals".' He acknowledges however (using the sexist language of the time) that it is sometimes used in the larger context of 'basic to human nature' or 'common to all men and cultures'. [9]

Further distinctions are made between 'specialities' and 'alternatives'. A pattern of behaviour attached to a particular group is called a speciality, while the degrees of choice are called 'alternatives'.

So presuming then that there are universals, what are they? what is their content? This is one of the sticking points in anthropology. A number do think that there are universals in the broader sense of the word although their number and genesis are not clear. According to Schreiter there is a 'growing consensus among cultural anthropologists that there may not be as many cultural universals as we had once hoped, that perhaps more of the cultural universals are in processes and modes of relationship than in content.'[10] Beals *et al* point out that although some universals can be identified it is not clear to what extent biological factors might explain them:

> ... comparison of existing human societies has led to the identification of a number of universals, but it is not known how closely these universals are linked to biological factors because there are other ways in which a human characteristic can become universal. [11]

Anthropologists have given different answers. For Joseph Greenberg[12] there is a series of characteristics of language that appear to be universal. Naom Chomsky sees it in the basic biological format that underlies all language. George Murdock says the nuclear family is universal or virtually universal. Others would point to the following two phenomena as universals or virtually so:

1. the tendency to divide labour and to organise societies in terms of age and sex, and

2. the incest taboos and exogamous rules affecting sexual relationships and patterns of intermarriage between brother and sister, father and daughter, or mother and son.

As was said above, one must distinguish between what is part of human nature and cultural patterns of behaviour. Culture is concerned with how people meet the needs of a common humanity. Rationality pertains to our common humanity and is not a universal since it is not learned. How one expresses rationality is learnt and is therefore cultural.

According to Geertz, who is a relativist in this regard, if you begin to compare, for example, what religion is in some groups as opposed to others, one soon realises that there is little in common - not enough to constitute 'religion'. Thus some of the white settlers in Australia concluded that the Aborigines did not have a religion.

Relativists tie culture to time, place and group. They assert that individuals unmodified by the customs of particular places do not in fact exist, have never existed, and most important, in the very nature of the case could not exist.[13] It is saying that 'the image of a constant human nature independent of time, place, and circumstance, of studies and professions, transient fashions and temporary opinions, may be an illusion, that what a man is may be so entangled with where he is, who he is, and what he believes that it is inseparable from them.'[14]

However others disagree with the relativists. Although culture obviously is tied to time, place and group, it does not exclude the idea of universals. They would argue that our common experience of different cultures throughout the world and the evidence of anthropologists themselves point to a common humanity which is in some limited cases expressed in universal patterns of behaviour.

Let us go back to the theories of culture now in a more or less historical and chronological way.

Theories of culture

The first was the **unilinear evolutionist** theory of anthropologists like E.B.Tylor (1832-1917), Lewis Morgan (1818-1881) and Sir James Frazer (1854-1941 of *The Golden Bough* fame, and Friedrich Engels (1820-1895). They saw culture as progressive and in a straight line from the lower to the higher, from the simpler to the complex, from the less moral to the more moral. Tylor believed culture is acquired by imitation, training and learning. Morgan maintained that culture started with savagery, moved on through barbarism to civilisation.

Although this theory has been debunked I find some elements make sense. For example, the fact that some primal peoples, e.g., the Melanesians, practised cannibalism and then later, under the influence of Europeans, modified their practices, indicates a kind of progress. The Mayan and Aztec civilisations 'progressed' to impressive construction skills, yet never discovered the wheel. On the other hand, there are many aspects of modern urban life, such as stress, pollution, pace of life, which I think, are retrogressive in term of primal societies. Progress is ambivalent to say the least. It has many dimensions, material, moral, physical and spiritual. Western society has undoubtedly advanced materially in terms of modern technology but can we say it has progressed spiritually after the Holocaust, Vietnam and the atrocities in Bosnia? (not to speak of the ordinary corruption in the institutions of our modern 'civilisation'.) Our observations of humanity show us that humans, as reflected in their culture, certainly do not advance in a unilinear way.

Franz Boas (1858-1942), the father of American anthropology, did not agree with this understanding proposing the **diffusionist** theory that culture originated in one place, e.g., ancient Egypt, and then spread throughout the world. He proposed that the concept of cultural relativism, that is, that there is not so much progression, as that all cultures have value and are different rather than better or worse. This concept still is very much present today and a most useful one indeed.

Again here, as with the evolutionists, I am inclined to say yes and no. It was not all diffusion if one thinks of the cultures of the Mayan and Aztec civilisations having achieved so much without contact with Egypt or the Middle East, at least as far as we know.

There was a resurgence of evolutionism in the 1940s by anthropologists like Leslie White (1900-1975, *The Evolution of Culture*, 1959) and Julian Steward (1902-1972, *Theory of Culture Change*, 1955), Childe and Marshall Sahlins, but this movement called **neo-evolutionism** declined in the 1960s. White had one theory in which I am interested and will pursue later. He emphasised the way in which members of a culture deal with environment and this determines the social and ideological aspects of culture. Culture, he pointed out, develops in direct response to technological 'progress'. Thus culture has three levels:

1. techno-economic,
2. social,
3. ideological.

A derivation of this idea was that of the cultural materialists who regarded the manner in which a people adapts culturally to its environment as the most significant factor in its development. I will take this up later in terms of responses to the environment on three different levels, the physical, social and ideational.

Next we have the **functionalists** who tried to relate aspects of culture to the function they played in that culture. They are represented by the Frenchman, Emile Durkheim (1858-1917) and the polish-born Bronislaw Malinowski (1884-1942).[15] I will return to Malinowski's 'needs theory' later because I find it very useful for our purposes. He did his fieldwork among the Trobrianders (an island off Papua New Guinea) and showed the interrelationship of elements in the culture. A weakness in his theory is that it was reductionist. It attempted to establish a one-to-one match-up between biological 'needs' and cultural response. As we know, not all responses are to a need and not all needs are biological. There are aesthetic, spiritual, emotional, intellectual and social needs to consider. Given that range, how does one know which needs are being responded to when there is a change from food-gatherers to crop producers? when music is made or created? when people drink kava?

Emile Durkheim painstakingly showed how the patterns of human social life are mirrored in their beliefs systems. His famous work, *The Elementary Forms of the Religious Life*, used the research of anthropologists among Australian Aborigines as data. His work has continued to be regarded as a classic in the literature although it has elicited much criticism. One is the (inevitable?) imposition of European categories on the data. For example his constant use of concepts such as 'the sacred and profane', 'supreme being', 'god', and 'religion'. It is easy to criticise after the event but he seems not to have been very conscious of his own interpretative framework as he worked through the data. And of course the very fact of having to use data collected and written up by others superimposed another interpretative layer to the problem. The way whites have allowed their own conceptual frameworks to influence their perception of Aboriginal beliefs is explored by T. Swain in his *Interpreting Aboriginal Religion* (1985) and in *A Place for Strangers* (1993) where he takes Micea Eliade to task for this tendency.

Functionalism was somewhat modified by the British anthropologist, Alfred Radcliffe-Brown (1881-1955[16] and called **structural-functionalism**. According to this theory each custom and belief has a specific function that serves to perpetuate the structure of that society, so that the society's continued existence is possible. This thrust in anthropology encouraged anthropologists to study cultures as systems. On the negative side it tended to negate the existence of any universal laws and left unanswered the question of why particular customs arise in the first place and what triggers change in a culture.

The Frenchman, Levi-Strauss (1908-) pursued another line, that of structuralism. He saw culture as an overt representation of underlying mental structures that have been affected by a group's physical and social environment as well as its history. Thus cultures vary considerably. This comes up in the question of the psychological differences between cultures. Whether some people think differently from another culture and perhaps have different mental biases. Do Africans have more music sense than other cultures and if so, is it genetic? As one can see, this leads into the areas of psychology and genetics. In passing, it can be noted that anthropologists like Ruth Benedict and Margaret Mead later carried on this tradition of a psychological approach to anthropology with some success.

The post World War II scene tended to be dominated by the **semiotic approach**[17] to culture exemplified in the Anglo-American group by Clifford Geertz, David Schneider, Victor Turner, Mary Douglas, Edmund Leach and Raymond Firth. Geertz is perhaps the trail-blazer among them. For example, he would have surprised Aristotle with his vision of humans as symbolising, conceptualising, meaning-seeking animals. He believes that human beings are suspended in webs of significance that they themselves have spun. 'I take culture' he says, 'to be those webs, and the analysis of it to be therefore not an experimental science in search of law but an interpretive one in search of meaning.'[18] One of his great contributions to the theme of this book was his article, 'Religion as a Cultural System' to which I will be returning.

Another dimension to culture is opened out by that multifaceted ideology known as Marxism. I will touch on just some of its dimensions here. We are familiar with its emphasis on material things as the defining element in human existence and its rejection of transcendent values and religion. If we think of culture as the more or less balanced interplay between technology, social organisation and ideology, then we can say that in Marxist theory, the economic factor is seen as the dominant one in a culture. In Marxism whoever controls the means of production, controls society. So Marx's comments on the genesis of human culture will come as no surprise:

> The mode of production of material life conditions the general process of social, political and intellectual life. It is not the consciousness of men that determines their existence, but their social existence that determines their consciousness .[19]

So the trick is to change people's social existence which is what the Bolshevik revolution set about doing. Ultimately after a period of class warfare the classless society or utopia would be ushered in. The second revolution of 1989 showed the world however that the theory of Marxism had not worked in practice and basically people were disillusioned with Marxism at least in Eastern Europe.

One of the positive things that Marxism has taught the west is that poor living conditions and human exploitation are ignored at society's peril. It also pointed out clearly that power is largely based on the ownership of the means of production and its distribution and that in any society, capitalist or communist, it can become a means of suppression and exploitation.

Let us return to the quote above. It is saying that human beings can rise above their social condition, can transcend their situation and determine to some extent their own consciousness. They are not slaves to the material world; they are not blind recipients of materialistic forces, even though from time to time, such forces might drag them down with its full weight of oppression. What the quote highlights is that people can contribute constructively to the critical reflection on existing social conditions and how they influence, rather than determine, human consciousness. Or, to use the framework of one theory of culture, Marxism holds that people can reflect on the physical, social and ideational environment and how they relate to these environments without being helpless victims to their forces. The Revolution of 1917 showed that some believed this.

A development of Marxist thinking is that of the Italian Marxist and philosopher, Antonio Gramsci (1891-1937). He emphasised the political angle to culture one might say. The ruling class, or dominant class, exercises great influence in any society. Gramsci introduced the concept of social hegemony and showed how the economic, political and cultural lives of people were intertwined and how, because of this, the ruling class subtly tried to impose their values, presenting an order of inequality and domination as if it were an order of equality and reciprocity. It was up to the working class to develop and maintain their culture in spite of, and in the face of, the social hegemony of the ruling class. Intellectuals had an important role to play in this scenario, according to Gramsci.

What he pointed out many years ago applies today. Williams has described this kind of hegemony. A powerful element of this is the particular and highly selective version of a people's history, 'a selective tradition' which is taught in the schools or expressed in television programs (witness the negative reaction in Australia to John Pilger's television programs that dared to present a different history; or the different versions of what happened in East Timor). Thus in Williams' words 'differential access to power is crucial in the determination of control over the means of cultural production, the means for the selection and presentation of tradition.'[20]

Definitions of culture

These theories give an outline, however brief, of some of the different emphases with regards to the approach to culture, the fundamental concept in anthropology. I would like to use some of these in scrutinising religion and its role in Australian culture. In doing this I would like to be eclectic also in my use of theories and definitions of culture since they are no more than the tools for unlocking insights. Let us start with some definitions of culture. I think they all have something to say about culture although I have no intention of discussing individually the more than three hundred definitions that exist!

Firstly, and on an elementary level, one can say simply that culture is something that embraces the whole of life. It is one's total social heredity, one's total tradition.

It covers all aspects of existence from the way one philosophises to the way one brushes one's teeth. It includes artefacts as well as intangibles (although some anthropologists, including Luzbetak, want to limit it to the intangibles). It includes sport, religion, art, music, motorcars, cuisine, fashions, etc. No aspect of life is excluded. Collectively all these elements form a culture. The deepening and development of this concept is seen by later anthropologists and we can trace this development through the definitions.

E.B.Tylor captures the breadth of the concept on the first level as I mentioned above. (Note the non-inclusive language of some of these definitions - which in itself is a reflection on the culture of the times in which they were written.) :

> Culture or civilisation is that complex whole which includes knowledge, belief, art, morals, law, customs, and any other capabilities and habits acquired by man as a member of society[21].

The comprehensiveness as well as this relativity of culture are well articulated by Franz Boas, who is keen to tie the concept back to a particular group:

> Culture embraces all the manifestations of social habits of a community, the reactions of all individuals as affected by the habits of the group in which he lives, and the products of human activities as determined by the habits.[22]

One can go a step further and include in the definition the ways one acquires culture, as does Lowie. He say that culture is:

> the sum total of what an individual acquires from his society - those beliefs, customs, artistic norms, food-habits, and crafts which come to him not by his own

creative activity but as a legacy from the past, conveyed by formal or informal education.[23]

What the above definitions emphasise then, is that culture is a way of life, 'a total plan for living' as Luzbetak keeps repeating. It is organised into a system and is acquired through learning. It is the way of life of a social group, not of an individual.

Others, like the structuralists, like to move from the visible aspects of culture and locate culture in the values that generate those artefacts and practices:

> Culture consists of the abstract values, beliefs and perceptions of the world that lie behind people's behaviour and that their behaviour reflects.[24]

There are many other ways of defining culture as Kapferer points out. He prefers the meaning-giving system that Geertz advocates so strongly. It is seen, he says, ' as a system of signs, a coherent order of meanings, an interpretative paradigm, a set of logical principles ingrained within and orienting social action'.[25]

Geertz's approach links up with what is called the 'integrative needs' theory (which is described below) which includes the development of a symbolic system of meanings. The symbols are essentially vehicles for meanings. Geertz's definition of culture is biased towards the symbolic system. He sees culture as:

> an historically transmitted pattern of meanings embodied in symbols, a system of inherited conceptions expressed in symbolic forms by means of which men communicate, perpetuate, and develop their knowledge about and attitudes to life.[26]

A symbol being any object, act, event, quality, or relation which serves as a vehicle for conception. The conception then becomes the 'symbolic meaning'. For example, the ritual act of the ANZAC Day ceremony has a symbolic meaning for the (dominant) Anglo-Celtic part of the community but might be meaningless to someone from Vietnam, Bosnia or the Sudan who has just arrived in Australia.

Culture is all of these things. It is the total way of life of a people. I do not like to see culture as only something in the mind. Luzbetak, following the semiotic lead, makes much of culture being in the mind like the blueprint for a house. It is not the house itself but only the blueprint. I prefer a more wholistic approach. I see it as including the artefacts and 'things' in a culture; as implying the values and thinking behind these things, and thirdly as also the system of signs and meanings that interpret reality for a people.

How does culture originate?

A definition of culture is all well and fine, but how, one may ask, did culture begin? In answering that question, one begins to deepen one's understanding of culture. One can look at the question from various viewpoints or theories. I would like to use two approaches. Both make sense to me in many ways, although not explaining everything. In my whole endeavour to link anthropology to religion I want to probe, test and propose what insights there might be without pretending to offer a master plan that solves all problems or explains everything. Paul Davies the physicist, often refers to the TOE (Theory of Everything) in his search for an explanation of the universe. Well, in anthropology there is certainly no TOE as yet.

Let us get back to the two approaches. The first way to look at culture is to invoke what Functionalists term the 'needs theory'.[27] In this approach culture is seen as meeting the basic needs of human beings. Malinowski was the first to speak of the threefold needs of people. These were identified as biological, instrumental and integrative needs. This theory was likewise reworked and appears now as *primary, derived* and *integrative* needs.

By *primary* needs are meant those basic needs such as the need for food, shelter, rest and waste removal from the body, health, expression of the sex drive and reproduction. In some cases all cultures come up with the same or similar solutions. Marriage (in some shape or size) is universal in being the answer to the sex drive and reproduction needs but the need for food is met in very different ways among the Eskimos, the Bushmen of the Kalahari and white Australians.

The second group of needs are those *derived* from the social nature of human beings. People have a need to come together and form friendship, hobby, sporting, learning, political, religious or industrial groups. When this happens structures and systems tend to form which then make up the profile of the social structure of a given culture. In Australia, for example, the need to form trade unions was felt early on this century and the movement developed so fast and so many of the work force became unionised, that it formed a distinctive part of Australian culture.

There are many derived needs and for the sake of brevity they could be categorised to include the need for:

• organisation of collective activity,
• communication,

- material satisfaction,
- social control,
- an educational system.[28]

Lastly *integrative* needs are identified as those which integrate some or many aspects of life. They do not arise from the physical, biological or social needs of people but flow from the intellectual and moral nature of human beings. Thus religion, literature, ethics, philosophy or art may integrate many aspects of life for some people helping them to bring meaning to such diverse things as birth, death, suffering, good and evil, sexuality and the purpose of life. Again, the *integrative* needs can be covered by saying they are the needs for:

- a feeling of right and wrong,
- expressing collective sentiment,
- a feeling of confidence,
- aesthetic expression,
- recreation.[29]

This 'needs theory' has the strength of showing how many elements of a culture fit together forming a kind of unity. But like most theories it does not answer all questions and the light it throws on aspects of culture is limited. Its main weakness is that it does not account for all aspects of culture nor for its inner dynamism. Are all expressions of culture a response to a need, or could it be a chance discovery, or something imported from another culture? Why when all needs are met, would a culture change? The 'needs theory' does not provide answers to questions like these.

The second approach to culture borrows from the neo-evolutionist White who spoke about three elements to culture, the *techno-economic, social* and *ideological*. His theory has been reworked and modified to present itself as the following statement: culture is the sum total of the human response to the environment. According to this theory the environment is threefold namely, *physical, social* and *ideational*. I believe it is better to combine the two approaches and say that culture meets the basic needs of people in a particular environment. Basic needs don't change but the environments in which they make themselves manifest do.

It follows that in a given culture a certain way of meeting a basic need in a particular environment could be very successful. However, if one changes the environment, the solution might be quite useless. Igloos are a good solution in the Arctic, but not much good in the Simpson desert!

Human beings learn to cope with the *physical* environment for example, by building homes for themselves to shelter from the cold. All cultures respond to this but not all in the same way. The Eskimos responded to the cold by building igloos; the Aborigines by using bivouacs and sometimes caves; in the United Kingdom, by building houses from stone with small windows to keep out the cold. Likewise each culture responds to the physical environment by finding food which it can eat, or producing food which the physical environment makes possible. (Aborigines can live off 'bush tucker', but Europeans often die in the bush because they have not had the time to adapt to the physical environment in terms of the need for food, i.e., to find out where the food is).

People respond to the *social* environment by developing kinship systems, family organisations, clubs and political parties. These become means whereby groups interact with each other to achieve social goals.

Thirdly a response to the *ideational* environment (that is, the world of ideas, values, feelings) by developing such things as knowledge, art, magic, literature, philosophy and religion. All cultures have built up some body of knowledge, collective experience and wisdom, and have given some meaning to life and its events.

Religion, being part of culture, is from one point of view, therefore, a learned response to the derived and integrative needs of individuals and groups. The group passes it down to the next generation. It is learnt by imitation and in both formal and informal ways. It becomes part of the individual's culture. This response will vary over the world. I will return to this in chapter 3 when discussing religion.

Summary

This chapter attempts to open up the conceptual field of anthropology by examining some aspects of what the discipline entails. The basic questions of the nature of anthropology, a common humanity and universals are discussed. Some different theories of culture (unilinear evolutionism, diffusionism, neo-evolutionism, functionalism, structural-functionalism, and semiotic theory) are outlined and followed up with an analysis of some selected definitions of culture which emphasise this or that aspect of culture. A view of culture that is all embracing is then adopted for this study: culture is a total way of life of a people. It includes the artefacts, values, ways of thinking and the sign system of a people. Finally, the important question of how culture originates is then pursued with the help of the needs theory (*primary*, *derived* and *integrative*) seen in the context of different environments (*physical, social* and *ideational*). Both these theories are adopted as having something to contribute about our understanding of culture and religious culture in particular, as we shall see in later chapters.

Points to ponder:

1. What arguments and examples can you find to contradict the unilinear evolutionist theory of culture?

2. Which of the theories of culture mentioned above appeals to you most. Why?

3. Do you believe in universal patterns of behaviour in all cultures? What evidence do you have?

4. What are the limitations of the 'needs' theory for the origin of culture?

2

How is culture acquired?

Once we have some idea of what culture is, an obvious consequent question that comes to mind is: *how does the individual acquire it?* This is what we need to investigate now. In summary form we can answer the question by saying that basically culture is acquired while growing up within a group of people in both formal and informal ways. It can be by imitation, formally through educational systems, or unconsciously by a process of cultural osmosis. Some technical terms used when talking about the transmission of culture need explaining.

Enculturation, diffusion and acculturation

The process whereby an individual learns the culture of the group into which he/she was born, is called enculturation and can occur only once in life. Although enculturation occurs only once it can be further subdivided into primary (initial) and secondary enculturation. Primary enculturation is active and non-retentive learning whereas secondary is active and reflective. This is necessary as the culture changes and individuals need this secondary learning to keep them up to date with their culture.

After enculturation other cultures can be learned only, or enforced, to a greater or lesser degree. This happens by *diffusion* and *acculturation*.

Firstly by *diffusion* is meant the spread of any culture by way of cultural items or elements. One adds to one's original culture by addition and modification. On the basic level of food the example of the pizza comes to mind. The Italian pizza has been diffused to many parts of the world. In Australia the pizza culture has been modified by the addition of pineapple - something unthinkable up until now. A different example of *diffusion*, taken from church life, would be the spread of scripture/prayer groups after Vatican II, or the music and prayer style of Taizé[30]. Boas was enthusiastic about diffusion because he believed it explained the evolution of cultures.

Acculturation is similar to diffusion with the qualification that it takes place on a much larger scale and frequently by coercion. It was used particularly in the context of the colonial powers, from the sixteenth century onwards, imposing their culture on the indigenous peoples. Whole cultures were forced to make massive changes to their way of life. Let me give some examples: the North American Indians were drawn into the fur trade; Aborigines into the white settler's social security system; the blacks of Southern Africa into the South African gold mining industry; some Indians into the sugar-cane industry in Fiji and Natal; Pacific Islanders into the copra plantations.

Azevedo refers to the expression *transcultural* phenomenon, that is, when there is a transference of cultural elements to almost all other cultures, while resisting their influence upon itself. There seems to be much overlap between his use of 'transcultural' and 'acculturation' with one difference being that the latter can occur between only two cultures and does not have to be global or near global. The spread of Christianity from the fifteenth century onwards would have to be seen as an example of a transcultural phenomenon as would the spread of modernity today.

Resistance to this kind of acculturation was sometimes very strong. For example, the European/capitalist way of thinking about money is basically acquisitive, whereas the African way is functional. Some Africans work to eat; sufficient funds dispense with the need to work. Christian missionaries sometimes thought indigenous peoples were short on faith if they did not convert to Christianity, but Luzbetak makes the point that this resistance showed precisely their strong faith in their own culture.

Acculturation can happen today if a developing country is swamped by western culture, or an industrialised country succumbs to an outside dominant culture, such as the American culture. The Irishman, Cardinal Moran offers a good example of voluntary acculturation, when on stepping ashore in Sydney in 1884, he declared, 'On this day I become an Australian, and I am determined to live as an Australian of Australia.'[31] History showed that it was not that easy!

It is useful to introduce here two other concepts which relate to culture and the contemporary world. They are *modernisation* and *modernity*. Azevedo has expressed it best. Modernisation, he says, is 'the process of transformation of the world as a result of increasing knowledge dynamically translated into technology'. From this comes modernity which refers to 'the resulting characteristics of the process in individuals, institutions, countries and cultures'.[32]

Another term to be mentioned in passing, is the term *inculturation* which is different to the preceding concepts. Broadly speaking, inculturation is applied to the process whereby the Christian gospel is adapted and applied to the culture in which it is preached. But it is more complex. Azevedo brings out clearly the essential two-way interaction between the culture and Christianity in his definition in which he sees inculturation as 'the dynamic and critically interactive relation between the Christian message and culture or cultures; an insertion of the Christian life into a culture; an on-going process of reciprocal and critical interaction and assimilation between them.'[33]

It is worth noting here that often today when we speak of inculturation it is not a simple interaction of the Christian message and a traditional culture. The 'culture' being considered is quite likely undergoing severe change from modernisation at the same time as it is trying to interact with Christianity. 'Modernity' represents a third culture. This is one reason why Azevedo uses the plural ('cultures') in his definition of inculturation.

I will return to this concept again in the context of the media and culture in chapter 6.

Symbiosis and socialisation

As regards the individual and the group, the learning of a culture is a *symbiotic* process. By that we mean the individual learns the culture from the group, their customs and their traditions, but the influence is two-way, that is, the individual can change the group culture by introducing some new customs which gradually become the norm. To quote an example of symbiosis using the pizza again: when the Australian Rugby Union player, David Campese was playing one winter in Italy he was able to get the local pizza restaurant to

add some pineapple to the pizza and then persuaded
others to eat it. It has now become part of the pizza
menu in that village!

A term that is used often in this context is *socialisation*.
What does it mean? Are enculturation and socialisation
the same? Not exactly. Enculturation embraces the
learning of all aspects of culture, including technology,
art, and religion while socialisation focuses on those
patterns of behaviour by means of which individuals
become functioning members of their social group,
adapt themselves to their fellow beings, achieve status
and acquire roles in society[34].

While the process of enculturation is going on, individuals are being taught how to cope with their primary, derived and integrative needs. The group/tribe
has worked out already how to cope with their needs
and passes its solutions on in the transmission of its
culture. Throughout the world different cultures have
come up with solutions, some of which are held in
common with other cultures, others unique. There is no
single, absolutely correct solution.

The relativity of culture

Where cultures are different it must be stressed that they
are not necessarily better or worse, simply different.
Culture is *relative*. This is most important. Its application
has enormous consequences for social harmony, especially in highly multicultural, or polyethnic, societies
like Canada, South Africa, the USA and Australia.

If the relativity of culture is not grasped, people will
label customs of other cultures as bad, stupid, or meaningless. In other words, ethnocentrism will prevail. It is

the culturally ignorant who say that the way they cope with the physical world is the best; the way they organise their social life is the best; their *Weltanschauung* is the most rational and intelligent. When one goes to Italy or Spain one might be inclined to think that a siesta after lunch is a crazy idea. With time one might be inclined to see that there is something in a siesta after all, and possibly one's own culture is a little crazy in working through the heat of the day.

When one begins to see that there are different ways of meeting certain needs in different cultures and that these ways are not necessarily better or worse than one's own, then one truly has begun to understand culture in an applied sense.

Let me give another example from the culture of the Aborigines which is very different from our western culture in terms of meeting primary, derived and integrated needs. John Harris refers to this incident between Aborigines and the missionaries in Queensland.[35]

The incident took place at Noonga Creek, (now Nundah, a suburb of Brisbane), a mission site of the German Lutherans in the early part of the nineteenth century. The missionaries planted vegetables over which they thought they had exclusive control as regards their use and usufruct. But the Aborigines helped themselves to the vegetables in spite of the protests of the missionaries. Now it happened that a tin dish was sounded to call the missionaries and their families to chapel, so the Aborigines came to the decision that they could best get the vegetables unmolested when the tin dish sounded!

The clash between the two cultures is clear to us now in hindsight. The western concept of the ownership of private property was ingrained deeply in the missionaries and has been part of our culture since at least medieval times. For the Aborigines the land and its fruits were there for the enjoyment of all. But the missionaries, not understanding Aboriginal culture, judged and condemned their action as stealing, applying the only yardstick they knew - western law as expressed in western culture.

Luzbetak cites the example of how Germans are shocked to see Americans eating corn on the cob because to the German corn is food for horses and pigs, not humans. Australians eat pork, beef, and rabbits, but little kangaroo. Some Asian cultures and some Indians of Mexico eat dogs. During the World War II, some people ate horsemeat in desperation. The Navaho Indians are nauseated by the very thought of eating something so slimy and smelly as fish, while the Aborigines on the coast use it as part of their normal diet. So each culture is different and as the saying goes, one person's meat is another person's poison. Ignorance of a culture unfortunately can lead to racism. The gold rush decade in Australian history led to Chinese (and other) immigration. There was naturally a lack of understanding of these cultures and the racism which grew out of this ignorance in the subsequent decades helped to create the environment in which the 1901 Commonwealth Immigration Restriction Act was passed.

But examples should be not only from eating habits. They come from all aspects of life. Some actions or behaviours in one culture can be perfectly acceptable but not so in another. Luzbetak has a humorous example from the time just after World War II in Japan when the USA government was intent on teaching the Japanese the value of democracy. One particular

American lecturer was particularly keen on showing by his behaviour what democracy meant in the classroom. He smoked, he took off his coat and finally he sat on the desk. At this the students rioted and left the room. In desperation the lecturer went to the administrator's office looking for an explanation. After consulting the students the administrator explained: 'Sir, in Japan table sacred; man's democratic bottom not!'[36]

But are all solutions simply passed on to the next generation? Are all individuals simply passive consumers of culture? Not at all. As we saw above, the relationship between the individual and group is *symbiotic*. The group might teach individuals to eat peas on the back of a fork, but when individuals grow old enough (and begin to reject or internalise value systems) they might change and start eating peas with the curved side of the fork, and (this is the important point) influence others to do the same - thus changing the culture in a slight way.

Culture is a network of interrelatedness

The phenomenological approach to culture could promote the idea that studying culture is like examining the dead parts of a corpse. Not so. Culture is not an interesting collection of discrete parts but a whole way of living, a dynamic process of interrelated parts, a 'system of meanings' in Geertz's language.

Sometimes the outside observer cannot see the interrelatedness. Only the insiders really know how their culture functions even if in an unconscious way. When insiders can explain their culture we refer to it as *native exegesis*. When it is not clear how a culture functions, one has to remain silent and observe. It is a question of studying the system of meanings operative in a culture and trying to relate this system to social structures and psychological processes. One cannot study a culture from a book and then say: I understand that culture. It is not something learnt quickly.

A good example of how a culture functions can be seen by taking one component of a culture (in this case the pig from Papua New Guinea) and shows its multiple meanings in that culture.

Luzbetak does this by pointing out that in Papua New Guinean culture the pig is intermeshed in every aspect of native life. The pig is the chief source of security. It is used in sacrifice to placate ancestors and win battles. Economically pigs are exchanged for the precious pearl shells and are a measure of family wealth. They often are the only source of protein and an exchange of pork seals friendships. Pork is essential to celebrations such as birth ceremonies, engagements and weddings. Pigs are necessary also for a boy to be initiated into a tribe and a woman's value as wife is measured by her skill in caring for pigs. Pigs also are an important part of bridewealth.[37]

In passing it might be noted how different the pig is in Jewish culture and how easily misunderstandings can occur when one comes to the scriptures from a cultural background that is totally different to the world of the Bible.

Before looking at Australian culture in particular, it might be useful to point out another distinction (mainly sociological) often made when speaking of culture: there is high Culture, (with an upper case 'C': opera, art, French cuisine, etc.), and low culture (with a lower case 'c': rock music, hot dogs, stockcar racing, etc.). Anthropologically speaking though, as we saw, culture embraces all aspects of life.

What is Australian culture?

The question suggests that there is an Australian culture. The answer however is complex and needs to be approached with sensitivity and care. I would want to begin my answer with a consideration of the oldest culture on this continent, and possibly in the world, the Aboriginal culture.

Aborigines have lived on Australian soil for more than fifty thousand years[38] and consist of many tribes scattered all over Australia. One should not speak of them as if they were one tribe and one culture. There were the tribes from the South-West, Western Desert, Central Desert, Lake Eyre, South-East, Cape York, Central North, Kimberleys, Torres Strait Islands, and Tasmania. Over three hundred languages were spoken. Australia prior to white settlement, was certainly not monocultural, and even less so, prior to World War II!

In spite of this there are some characteristics that Aboriginal tribes seem to share: great respect for the land, strong kinship ties, a sacramental view of the material world, belief in the spirit world as close to us, faith in the community/tribe, viewing life as integral. They had met their primary, derived and integrative needs in a given physical, social and ideational environment. They had a culture, or better, each tribe or grouping had its own culture.

In looking at the origins of Aboriginal and Anglo-Celtic culture in Australia, it is worth asking to what extent the development of culture was the outcome of a symbiotic relationship between the physical environment and people concerned. I would like to explore this now as it seems to be an important part of Australian culture.

As Luzbetak points out, the way people respond to the environment is called cultural ecology and originally promoted by Steward and Sahlins and later on by others like Vayda, Rappaport, Harris, Longacre, Meggers and Flannery[39] We can take it a step further and also take into account the way a people effects the environment, hence the symbiotic designation for the relationship.

Applying this approach, one can affirm the role of the landscape in cultural formation. The abundant berries, fruits, nuts, meat (animals) and fish meant that the Aborigines could live off the land. From the animal life they gathered the ideas for their totems (the kangaroo, fish, serpent). The size of the land and sparse population meant they could be nomads rather than agriculturists.

How has the landscape shaped the culture of the white settlers? They have clung mainly to the coast because the interior was too harsh and dry. The beaches on the other hand were beautiful and the coastal strips with good rainfall provided crops and grazing for stock. This led to the leisure activities associated with the beach like swimming, life-saving, sunbathing, nude bathing, surfing and windsurfing, as well as those associated with farming. For some, Christmas day even is celebrated on the beach. The heat and searing light resulted in some people in the Outback speaking with semi-closed eyes and mouth as protection against the light and flies. The good weather also favours outdoor activities of which the barbecue has become the symbol. But there are many: picnicking, bushwalking, orienteering, bird-watching, flying, hang-gliding, and, of course, the general team sports like netball, rugby, football, cricket, hockey, etc. Living mostly on the eastern seaboard, watersports in particular have become a very distinctive descriptor of Australian culture.

Let me take one sport to illustrate the interplay of people and physical environment further. Golf is popular for a number of reasons. The combination of abundant space and good weather allows it to thrive whereas in Japan, the premium on space and the exorbitant cost of a round of golf restrict its growth.

The fact that the country is huge (and originally thought by the whites to be empty) has led to building many bungalow houses, that is, houses of a single storey on a quarter-acre block. This, as opposed to highrise building patterns in other countries, means that people get used to living with a lot of space between them. One, of course, gets used to this and does not notice it. It has militated against a sense of community and promoted a more individualistic and perhaps more selfish way of life. However, with the arrival of so many boat people from South East Asia in Australia, one hears often how they have severe psychological problems in trying to adapt to the few people living apart, having come from (what we would say) the overcrowded cities of South-East Asia.

On the other hand, what influence has the culture of the people had on the landscape? As regards the Aborigines, the question is put the wrong way round. It was the land that formed the people. As Swain has shown, the Aboriginal ontology was a locative one as opposed to an Utopian one, that is, one embedded in the land, in place rather than time.[40] They belonged to the land which formed them and claims them. When they die they return to the place of their origin. Therefore there was collaboration with, rather than domination of, nature. Even their rejection of becoming an agricultural society which was possible as a result of their contact with Melanesian culture according to Swain, could have been due to their view of the land. Agriculturists work the land and by virtue of the effort they put into it, they get to 'own' the land. The Aborigines are owned already by the land and live off the fruits of the land.

Not so with the white settlers. Part of their European culture was the domination and utilisation of nature. To some extent this was anchored in their interpretation of Genesis 1:28 where it speaks of dominating the earth and happens to dovetail perfectly with an exploitative colonial mindset. The fact is that in two hundred years the white settlers and their descendants have chopped down half the forests in Australia, impoverished the soil through overgrazing, scarred the countryside looking for minerals, through urbanisation polluted the air and water with chemicals and, generally, made a mess of the environment. A belated ecological awareness is trying to right these wrongs of the past.

Having said so much for the symbiotic relationship between the physical environment and the people, what else can be said about the dominant cultures? The Anglo-Celtic dominant culture is usually characterised by hedonism, materialism (a point emphasised by Bruce Wilson in his writings), leisure loving, mateship, laid-backness, and sport-madness. Much of this is impressionistic and it is extremely difficult to separate the myth from the reality. Some of the myths have been debunked by our knowledge of Australian society today.

Tony Kelly has identified some relevant limit-situations which could help in the process of determining Australian culture. The limit-situations he identifies are: isolation, Aborigines, affluence, migrants, leisure, sexuality, and the land.[41] By finding out what the majority of Australians thinks and feels about these topics, one will begin to understand the mental thinking patterns of the people in the culture.

The social commentator and researcher, Hugh Mackay[42] speaks of the values that still inform Australians, such as the family and a job. He speaks of the disillusionment of the nineties and a concomitant call for a return to basics. In describing Australian culture today, Mackay points out several changing areas of culture that require redefinition. One is the appearance of feminism with its ensuing considerations about the working mother, fatigue, the burden of guilt, the male response and changes in sexual relationships. Each of these needs time and discussion. What is clear is that the culture is changing. It is an upheaval in secular society as big and significant as Vatican II was for Catholicism and perhaps the ordination of women in Anglicanism.

Another change in the culture is the cluster of issues associated with marriage: co-habiting, divorce, blended families, in-laws and out-laws. And yet in spite of all this, Mackay reports: 'And yet, while acknowledging that it is much harder to define what a family actually is than it used to be, Australians seem just as keen on the idea of the family as ever. As the reality of family life becomes less stable, the ideal seems to become even more attractive.'[43] Australians have hit the nail on the head, for family is indeed vital to society as Moira

Eastman has demonstrated in her study.[44] Drawing on studies in the USA and in Australia, she emphasises the importance of the family in the promotion of the individual's competence, spontaneity, self-esteem, confidence, energy, intelligence and co-operation.

Mackay describes how the work scene has changed dramatically since the near full employment of the sixties. He also draws attention to the way Australians have become a people living beyond their means while simultaneously developing an underclass. Migrants are conditionally welcomed. The myth of mateship does not extend often to people of other sub-cultures. Politically the party distinction has become blurred, Labor having won over much of the middle Australia formerly going to the Liberals. Furthermore Australians today do not like political commitment. They prefer a certain cynicism and a freedom to keep their options open.

In short, he says that Australia is going through a sort of adolescence with an identity crisis. Already there is a backlash with a certain back-to-basics movement, as well as the extreme wing of fundamentalists (again, religion mirrors this movement).

The last section in chapter 4 of his book, Mackay has entitled, *Back to the Tribe*, outlining the felt need to create a sense of community within a society. There is a movement to emphasise group identity and unity rather than diversity and fragmentation which have characterised the past twenty years or so. The environment becomes one such rallying point; others are the family and family values, the neighbourhood, a search for a national identity, and in religious terms, both the desire for Christian unity and the wish for the healthy interfaith relationships. Mackay has given us much food for thought and a realistic appreciation of where Australian culture has come from and the direction it is taking.

Reflections on these topics may lead to modification of behaviours and this could be a positive thing in the development of the Australian character. Attitudes towards Aborigines is a good example. In the light of the Mabo decision white Australians now have the opportunity of being reconciled with black Australians in acknowledging the lie of *terra nullius*. Other limit-situations likewise may give the opportunity for positive attitudes to develop.

A.G. Stephens said in 1904 that there is in our culture, 'a sceptical and utilitarian spirit that values the present hour'.[45] This refers to the hedonism and pragmatism that some commentators point out. Someone has said that sanctity is very un-Australian, yet the culture has produced people like Mary MacKillop, Caroline Chisholm, Damien Parer, Bede Polding, Flynn of the Outback, Ted Noffs, Fred Hollows. With the beatification of Mary MacKillop the thinking, and thus the culture, might be modified.

Other ethnic groups in the Australian community have subcultures which reflect partly their country of origin and partly their adaptation to a new culture. They could be called subcultures, that is, they share some things in common with the dominant culture, while others are unique to their cultural group. Thus we have for example, the Italian, Greek, Maltese, Samoan, Tongan, Vietnamese, Laotian, Cambodian, Chinese, Filipino subcultures.

Figure 1

The culture / subculture relationship

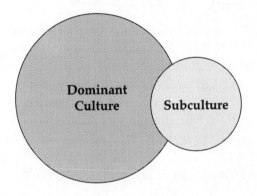

Culture is dynamic and changing.

I said above that culture is alive, implying that culture changes. Let me illustrate by referring to Aboriginal culture. Some scholars were inclined to see Aboriginal culture before white contact as unchanging, as part of a romantic idea of a primal society, of an ageless traditional culture. Swain however sets out in *A Place for Strangers*[46] to show that quite likely the influence of outsiders (Melanesians, Mocassans, Timorese) changed their culture (more specifically, their ontology) even before the arrival of Europeans. Growth and change is a rule of life. All cultures change over time. It is a myth to think that some 'traditional' cultures are above change. Some aspects of change have been mentioned already, e.g., diffusion and acculturation imply change. Perhaps it is time to make some further distinctions.

Changes can arise from within the culture itself, in which case we speak of *origination*. When the change arises from outside the culture we speak of *diffusion* or *acculturation*. Both these concepts are primary process-es in so far as they initiate changes which might be rapid (revolution) or gradual (long-term, cultural drift or his-toric accident).

People are often reluctant to change and old ways persist. There are, according to anthropologists, three kinds of persistence: *general*, *sectional* (only certain aspects of a culture), or *partial* (a custom carried out with reduced frequency, like the wearing of the *hijab* only by certain Muslim girls in Australia). Elements of a culture that have, with the passage of time, changed their function and become mere conventions (like colouring Easter eggs) are called 'survivals'.

There is another aspect to consider about cultural change. If one considers the object of the change, it could be:

• substituted (the vernacular for Latin in Catholic liturgy; receiving communion in the hand instead of on the tongue),
• lost with no replacement, like young Catholics not praying the rosary, or young Muslims not praying five times a day,
• incremented, that is, added to the culture, like television
• fused to what is already there, as in the case of Pidgin English or Fanigalo.

The process of change consists usually in

• the primary or innovative process that gives rise to the change,
• the secondary or integrative step that attempts to fit the change into the culture,
• the terminal stage when things settle down, that is, reach a stage of equilibrium.

The repercussions of Vatican II for example, have not really reached the terminal stage yet in many parts of the world. The changes in information and technology (modernisation) seem so rapid that the stage of settling down never seems attainable.

Let us return to the Australian scene. Above we identified the high unionisation in Australia as (partially) an expression of response to the social needs of people. However in the last few years, the trade unions have been going through a process of change due to the change in the work culture. As unionisation declines, other responses to social needs will be found, or perhaps have been found already.

A clear example of change from without, by acculturation (with coercion in this case), could be taken from a completely different sphere of life, namely religion. Catholics in Australia (and elsewhere) had enormous changes thrust on them from without, from the Vatican, through the Council known as Vatican II. True some people in Australia might have supported all these changes, but most would not have understood what was going on. Cardinal Gilroy, on leaving for the Council, told reporters that he thought it would be all over in a month! (it took more than three years!) The element of coercion was clearly there. Parish priests were told to turn their altars around, do away with communion rails, use the vernacular and speak eye-to-eye to the congregation. This major event has changed the religious culture of Catholics dramatically. Many have not been able to appropriate these changes. I will return to this dramatic example in chapter 5.

Other changes from without are the numerous migrant groups who have added to the cultural mix of Australia. They have brought some of their culture to bear gradually on the dominant culture while at the same time they have become integrated into the dominant culture in other ways. The process is symbiotic by nature.

An example of the first is the obvious one of how the Australian cuisine has become multicultural. A walk through the large cities will provide overwhelming evidence of this. Examples of the second type of change can be seen in looking at that traditional, obscure, Anglo-Celtic sport called cricket. It used to be played by people with only Anglo-Celtics names. Now the penetration of other cultures into Australian culture can be seen by the appearance of names from other cultures: Pascoe (Yugoslavia), Chee Quee (Chinese), Valetta, Divenuto (Italian) in cricket and Vidmar, Talay, Markovski, Spyridakos, Petkovic, Mendez and Ryschka in soccer. Doubtlessly there are many other examples from other areas of life, be it film, art, tennis, netball, or whatever.

Looking at Australian culture overall, it is now more accurate to speak of Australian cultures (in the plural), or subcultures, although the dominant culture since white settlement was, and remains, Anglo-Celtic. This might not be the case in fifty to a hundred years hence.

Is Australian culture a secular culture?

Bruce Wilson, in his *Can God Survive in Australia* (1983), argues that the decline in church attendance is the inevitable result of industrialisation and secularisation. Religion is seen as irrelevant to people's lives. From being central it is now a private affair. Religion is one choice among many today.

It was noted that religion plays the role of giving meaning to life, of bringing together all that is important in life. On the ideational level it provides the intellectual linkages of all parts of culture. Does religion still play this role in Australian culture?

**Does Religion still provide the linkages
in Australian culture?**

What is meant by a secular society? Does secular mean less frequent church attendance? Does it mean the separation of the religious dimension of life from the political, economic, social? (the process of secularisation). This latter is what Vatican II spoke about when it recognised the legitimate autonomy of the political, economic and any other sphere of life. So in itself it is a positive and good process. One could say that the shift has been from a religious view of life in the Middle Ages to a critico-scientific view of life by way of the Enlightenment through into modern and postmodern times. Azevedo defines secularisation succinctly as 'the attempt to give rational explanations to natural phenomena as well as the predominance of immanence over transcendence'.[47]

When, however, secularisation does this to the exclusion of God entirely from life, that is, denies the religious dimensions and the existence of God, it is called *secularism*. This characterised the communist totalitarian states. Believers see secularism as a perjorative term. The word secular is often used with a neutral connotation. For example: the secular world of commerce goes about its business; public institutions are all secular. One can speak also of secular and religious rites of passage without implying any judgment.

When, however, it is said: 'Australia is a secular society', one feels that a certain negative judgment is made. It is used in the sense that people are neglecting their religious duties. It is used as a kind of ideological tool for beating people. It is generally so broad a generalisation that it is fairly useless in helping anyone to understand the society in which we live.

Let us return to the census statistics for a moment. Some point out the rise in the number of Australians who answered the census questionnaire about religion with a 'no-religion' response as proof that Australia is a secular society. I do not think it is that simple. Firstly, 'No religion' is relatively small percentage (12.9 per cent in 1991, as opposed to 0.4 per cent in 1911) and particularly strong among the 20-39 age group; secondly there is no saying what people intended by this answer. It does not necessarily mean that they have no religious beliefs. (The National Social Science Survey showed that only a quarter of those who said they had no religion said also that they did not believe in God.) Do those who say they have no religion mean no institutionalised religion? Many would agree that the crisis today is not in the message of Christianity but in the institutions.[48] Certainly this response in the census cannot be invoked as evidence of a secular society.

Mention must be made also of those who answer the 'No Stated Religion' category (10.2 per cent in 1991 and 2.7 per cent in 1911). Many explanations are possible here. It may mean a lack of interest in religion; or simply a preference not to answer any question that they do not have to; some may feel their religious beliefs have nothing to do with the state. Overall they tend to be the Anglo-Celtic part of the population (two-thirds) rather than people from a language background other than English (LBOTE). It cannot be said that this category provides evidence for the statement that Australia is a secular society.

Summary

The acquiring of culture has been examined in this chapter with the help of the critical concepts of enculturation, diffusion, acculturation, inculturation, symbiosis and socialisation. The relativity of culture is seen as most important for promoting positive attitudes towards different peoples and races. This is illustrated with examples. Further examples show how all aspects of a culture are interrelated and how thoroughly culture permeates a community's life. Having said all that, a few aspects of Australian culture are discussed and analysed with some suggestions as to what the distinctive aspects might be. The chapter concludes with a consideration of religion in Australia and whether the census figures allow one to say Australia is a secular society.

Having looked at some key concepts in anthropology in chapters 1 and 2, it is now time to move on and reflect on 'religion' in the next chapter. This will enable us to outline an anthropological framework of culture and religion which can be used implicitly and explicitly in subsequent chapters.

Points to ponder:

1. Give examples of how the physical environment of Australia influences the food that the Aborigines and white population produce/eat.

2. Can you think of examples from Australian culture where the symbiotic nature of culture is evident?

3. Think back on your childhood. Describe how you acquired your culture and especially your religious culture. What were the values and the customs/practices you learnt? How did you learn them?

4. One speaks about the interconnectedness of the components in a culture. In Australian society how important and what is the meaning of the motorcar? Money? One's job? House?

5. Do you think the symbiotic relationship between landscape and people is valid? If so, what other examples can you give?

6. How is the religious culture of the Middle Ages different to that of the modern scientific world. Why and how did it change?

3

What is religion?

I can recall with amusement the time a parent was discussing with me the type of school she would like her children to attend. I can say truthfully that this parent was profoundly uninformed and her approach simplistic. She was trying to say that somehow she felt a church-related school was a good choice for her children. In the state schools, as she saw it, there are teachers who are very politically-minded, whereas in church-related schools they are religiously-minded. She ended off with the succinct conclusion: 'I would rather my child was mixed up in religion than mixed up in politics'!

This parent obviously saw religion and politics as being very separate. Many would see it differently. The point is that people disagree about the precise meaning of the word 'religion' (and 'politics' too). There is no unanimity as to what is included and what excluded by the term. So for the moment let us focus on what religion is and the different ways one could be 'mixed up' in religion.

Philological meaning of 'religion'

The origins of the actual word *religion* are rather obscure,[49] and there is no agreement. The Latin word *religio* could have come from any of the following possible sources:
1. according to Cicero, from the Latin, *relegere*, mean-

ing *to turn to constantly, observe conscientiously* or *to reread or deepen one's knowledge*. So it could make sense, in that religion is frequently and consciously turning to your gods, whatever they may be; or a deepening of one's knowledge about the more profound things of life.

2. according to Lactantius and Augustine, *religari,* meaning *to bind oneself back, to connect or join*. Bouma favours this meaning and sees religion as connecting the present life with the future, the supernatural with the natural, the transcendent with the immanent, the here and now with the beyond.[50] On the practical level, religion could be said to bind one back to the household gods, be they Roman, Greek, Jewish or Australian.

3. *reeligere,* meaning *to choose again*, possibly in the sense that as one grows up one chooses again as to one's beliefs. It could mean to commit oneself with renewed commitment or to appropriate one's religious tradition.

'If ever you get mixed up with religious people, Mrs Green, God 'elp yer!'

Mixed up in Religion

To me the first two seem the more plausible although the third does bring home the idea of an adult commitment later in life to a fundamental aspect of life. Perhaps this was something often seen in ancient Rome. Certainly some of the early Christians were pagans who 'chose again' as regards their gods. All of them have overtones of something which unites, or integrates one's life; something which is an underpinning for life.

In cultural terms one might say religion is an aspect of life that integrates needs, or provides a response to the ideational environment or provides a system of meaning to one's life.

Religion is a complex reality

Religion has many faces, not all of which are apparent to the casual observer. It is said that academics always start a discussion on a given topic with a definition. Be that as it may, a discussion of definitions does open up the concept and shed light on the finer points.

Let me say at the outset that, as with culture there is no one answer or definition. Theologians' definition of religion might well assume the existence of God and faith, and this colours their statements. Atheists like Marx do not work with the hypothesis of a god, so their definition of religion is couched in quite different terms. The social scientists, such as anthropologists who claim not to be driven by any ideology (except that of being objective!), can take either a phenomenological approach and simply observe and describe what they see while bracketing questions of meaning, or they could suggest, like Geertz, that the important thing about religion is the interpretation of actions that are being performed.

But let us go back to the question of how we study religion. Basically there are two ways:

1. That of scientists or observers who stand *outside the faith perspective* and study it as would any scientists, employing the methods of a particular scientific discipline, such as psychology, sociology, philosophy or anthropology. They try to be objective, although past studies such as the one of the Aborigines by Durkeim, show that it is impossible to be entirely objective. This approach, which scientists or observers would take, can be described as:

objective
non-confessional
polythmethodological

2. That taken from *within a faith tradition*. However, while it is more subjective, confessional and focused on theological method, when theologising it is more and more beginning to take into consideration data from other sciences. This approach, which theologians would take, can be described as:

subjective
confessional
using a variety of theological methods.

Different kinds of definitions

Bearing in mind this basic orientation to the study of religion, one may enquire about defining what exactly religion is. Here it is helpful to recall the different kinds of definition that might be used. Habel and Moore make a useful distinction between various kinds of definitions of religion thus:

essential definitions (trying to capture the essence of religion),
functional definitions (the role that religion plays),
definitions by *examples* (a given religion 'is like' Judaism or Christianity),
phenomenological definitions (describing what appears in front of you as religion), and
typological definitions (emphasise the generic types of religions and religious phenomena).[51]

These different kinds of definitions are a good guide to understanding how individuals come to quite different insights into religion. Later we will ask ourselves what definition of religion the white settlers in Australia in the eighteenth century had in mind when they concluded that the Aborigines had no religion? What did the governors mean when they said they were in favour of religion? What do politicians mean when they say that religion and politics should be kept separate?

Let me show how some classic definitions of religion relate to the kinds of definitions just listed. I will not say much about the typological approach because it is close to the phenomenological nor about the definition by example which is self-evident.

The liberal Protestant philosopher, Friedrich Schleiermacher (1768-1834) defending religion against the rationalism of the Enlightenment, thought the essence of religion was the *Abhängigkeitsgefühl* - the feeling of absolute dependence on God, thus touching on an important psychological and emotional dimension of religion. He referred to it as 'the solemn music which accompanies all human experience'.[52]

Rudolph Otto (1869-1937), professor of theology at Marburg and promoter of the comparative study of religions, wrote a book, *The Idea of the Holy*,[53] (in German, *Das Heilige*). In it he sees the essence of religion as the sense of the sacred or the *numinous* (from the Latin, *numen* = an expression of the will or might of the deity). This numinous experience is a *mysterium tremendum et fascinans - a mystery filled with awe and also fascinating.* God is seen as *Das Ganz Andere*, ('the wholly other'). The subtitle of his book sums it up well, 'An Inquiry into the non-rational factor in the idea of the divine and its relation to the rational'. He was looking for the essence of religion and found it in the 'holy' dimension.

Another essentialist definition which has proved popular is that of Protestant theologian, Paul Tillich (1886-1965). He saw religion as being a system of beliefs and practices directed at the ultimate. Religion is about matters of ultimate concern, that is, those beyond the here and now. He saw God as Being-itself, not one being among others, and thought all other statements about God as symbolic. Sociologists have taken to this idea of ultimacy and use it to distinguish between religious and non-religious meaning systems.

Matters of ultimate concern

Karl Marx (1818-1883), on the other hand, building on insights from Feuerbach, expresses his idea of religion in functional terms. Religion, he said, is like a drug. It is the opiate of the people - something that takes people's minds off the injustices of this world. The pie-in-the-sky preaching of religion is an illusion, but at least it helps people for the moment to bear the suffering of this life. Religion has its function but it does not bring happiness. For that a revolution is necessary.

Ninian Smart's approach is that of a phenomenologist. He did not so much provide a definition as outline a framework for the study or description of religion. He saw religion as having six dimensions. These he called the *ritual, mythological, doctrinal, ethical, social* and *experiential* dimensions.[54] They have proven to be a most practical way for a phenomenologist to describe, (or for a student to study), any religion or sect.

Remaining within the general concept of functionalism, the discipline of psychology has provided some very rich and useful insights. The psychologist Freud, in his *The Future of Illusion* (1928) described religion as a 'universal obsessional neurosis'. Jung however was more positive about religion. He spoke about religious archetypes or images common to our collective unconscious. He claimed that none of his patients had been healed properly until they had acquired a religious outlook on life. That is a very powerful statement coming from one with his experience of humankind.

Other psychologists such as Gordon Allport, A.H. Maslow and Rollo May stress that religion is a positive force in helping to produce a properly integrated personality better able to achieve desired goals.

Any definition takes into account the particular interests of the discipline out of which the investigator comes. Take sociology for example. Bouma's definition of religion is a good example of this. He says religion is *'a shared meaning system* which grounds its answers to questions of meaning in the postulated existence of a greater environing reality and its related set of practices *and social organisation.'*[55] (italics added). We can hear the sociologist speaking in this definition.

Moralists are often inclined to see religion, in an essentially reductionist way, as connected with morality. For Furphy religion was the sermon on the mount and for other Christians it is often the ten commandments - both referring to moral actions. Perhaps that is why James McAuley said some Australians mistake morality for genuine religion.

Is religion a product of culture?

It is easy enough for anthropologists to see religion as the product of culture since that is their particular interest and perspective. Culture is a human construct as we saw in chapters 1 and 2, and hence religion, which is one aspect of culture, is a human construct too. However one does not expect a theologian to echo the same approach. That is why the ideas of Barth to whom I now want to turn, are so interesting.

The Swiss Calvinist theologian, Karl Barth (1886-1969) is interesting because of the emphatic distinctions he makes and the extreme position he holds on the topic of religion. This makes him stand out among the theologians and throws into relief the difference between Christian faith and religion - at least from the viewpoint of Christian believers.

In general in his theological writings Barth stressed the absolute difference between God and human beings, between a person's given state of sinfulness and God's revelation and grace. He reacted strongly to liberal Protestantism which he saw as selling out to human learning and forgetting the uniqueness of revelation through Jesus Christ. With this orientation let us now consider some of Barth's ideas on religion.

In his writings Barth, more often than not, uses the word 'religion' in a perjorative sense. He frequently refers to religion as a human-made thing as opposed to divine revelation through Jesus Christ. He protested, for example, against the 'arrogance of religion, by which men, speaking of God from the welter of their experiences, mean in fact themselves'.[56]

A collection of some of his references to religion in his *Epistle to the Romans* and from his *Church Dogmatics* will give a good insight into his thinking. He saw the dangers of religion as killing the truth: 'Instead of pointing beyond itself, it may be erected, like some great pyramid, as an immense sepulchre within which the truth lies mummified in wood and stone.'[57] He insisted that religion remains a human achievement[58]; '...the supreme sin of religion, the sin of anthropomorphism' [59]; religion is like a drug - instead of 'counteracting human illusions', it introduces 'an alternative condition of pleasurable emotion'[60] ; religion must die. In God we are rid of it.[61]

Finally he says something positive about religion if only in a very guarded way: '... religion is a human possibility, and consequently, a limited possibility, which by its ineffectiveness, establishes and authenticates the freedom of God to confer grace upon men.'[62]

In essence Barth says there is a lot of idolatry, self-righteousness, unbelief, hollowness and emptiness, and self-centredness in human religion - the exact opposite to divine revelation. By human religion human beings attempt to justify and to sanctify themselves before a capricious and arbitrary picture of God[63]. 'Man's attempt to know God from his own standpoint are wholly and entirely futile'[64] He rejects 'religion' as humans' initiating a relationship with God, or the construction of an idol to human excellence and perfection.

Barth counterposes revelation as the 'true' religion which must replace the human construct, religion. Barth explains the concept 'religion' thus:

> (there is) No 'true' religion. It is only the revelation of God through Christ that is true. Religion can only become true, i.e., according to that which it purports to be and for which it is upheld. And it can become true only in the way in which man is justified from without, that is, not of its own nature and being, but only in virtue of a reckoning and adopting and separating which are foreign to its own nature and being, which are quite inconceivable from its own standpoint which came to it quite apart from any qualifications or merits. Like justified man, religion is a creature of grace. But grace is the revelation of God. No religion can stand before it as true religion.'[65]

By 'religion' Barth means anthropological or phenomenological religion discovered in the era of modernity. He criticises Protestant theologians for exchanging 'revelation' for 'religion'.[66] They subordinate revelation to religion.

Barth in his descriptions of religion parallels in many ways the language and insights of today's anthropologists and phenomenologists. He sees religion as an area of human knowledge and experience. Religion is always there 'as one specific area of human competence, experience and activity, as one of the worlds within the world of men'[67]. He thus anticipates the way phenomenologists see religion today : it is a human phenomenon.

What does anthropology say about religion?

Anthropologists affirm at least some of what Barth was saying, that is, religion is a product of human culture. Within this general approach there are nuanced stances among anthropologists.

There are those whose approach to religion is developmental and parallels their evolutionist approach to culture in general. They see religion as a manifestation of a very primitive stage of humankind, something human beings would grow beyond as they progressed on the human ladder. Tylor saw it as a barbaric form of mentality defining it simply as 'belief in spiritual beings'.[68] Lucien Levi-Bruhl thought religion is pre-logical in the stage of humankind's development. If so then humankind is taking a long time to develop because religion is still there!

Marxism has tried for seventy years to eradicate religion in the former USSR and elsewhere, but it persists. J.G. Frazer, who was also an evolutionist, was no less disparaging of it. He saw sympathetic magic as religion's chief characteristic.

Not surprisingly, Malinowski, who was a functionalist, took a more pyschological/functional approach. He said that religion helped one to endure 'situations of emotional stress by open(ing) up escapes from such situations and such impasses as offer no empirical way out except by ritual and belief into the domain of the supernatural'[69] (a functional definition.) His functional approach is clear from the following:

> ...magic and religion are not merely a doctrine or a philosophy, not merely an intellectual body of opinion, but a special mode of behaviour, a pragmatic attitude built up of reason, feeling, and will alike. It is a mode of action as well as a system of belief, and a sociological phenomenon as well as a personal experience.[70]

One of his major contributions to anthropology was his essay, 'Magic, Science and Religion'[71] in which he detailed the distinctions between these concepts. Magic, he said, is an attempt to give humans the power over certain things, to control forces greater than the individual through set formula, while religion is an acknowledgment of humankind's impotence in the face of forces greater than itself. Both arise out of situations of emotional stress such as crises in life, death, initiation into tribal mysteries, unhappy love or unsatisfied hatred.

Micea Eliade, who was really an historian of religions rather than an anthropologist, disagreed with Claude Levi-Strauss who said that myths told us something only about the social setting of those who use them. Eliade on the contrary, saw the highly significant religious side to myth. Myth he regarded as an alternative mode of thinking to conceptual discourse: there is something profound in the myths that people hand on. On the connection between myth and practice, earlier anthropologists like Malinowski and Leach saw a direct link but Levi-Strauss saw myth more as a commentary on those who composed them.[72] However today it seems the etiological and normative functions of myths vary and make generalisations a risky business.

But a big change came in anthropology after World War II with the work of the American anthropologist Clifford Geertz. This move to culture as a system or pattern of symbols which make meaning has dominated anthropology and flowed onto considerations of religion.

The theme of suffering is not far from any definition of religion. As Geertz remarked: 'With the possible exception of Christian Science, there are few if any religious traditions, "great" or "little", in which the proposition that life hurts is not strenuously affirmed, and in some it is virtually glorified.'[73] It is not surprising that he includes this reflection in his description of religion.

Geertz has described religion from the viewpoint of cultural anthropology in his article, entitled 'Religion as a Cultural System'.[74] In it he gives us a theoretical framework for the understanding of religion from the viewpoint of cultural anthropology. In it he depicts religion as a symbolic system. Symbol is taken in a very broad sense. It can mean any object, act, event, quality, person or relation used as a vehicle for a conception and that conception becomes the symbol's meaning. Religion, according to Geertz, is a system of symbols brought together to help humankind cope with the chaotic forces of life that render people impotent in the analytic, emotional and moral sense. In Javanese culture, Geertz points out, because 'religion' explained everything about life, it was the same word as 'science'.[75]

His point of departure is that sacred symbols function to synthesise a people's ethos. (By ethos he means a people's worldview, together with the tone, character, quality of their life and its aesthetic and moral styles.) When events happen in life which people are unable to analyse, bafflement follows; when emotional impotence prevails it leads to pain, and moral impotence to moral paradox. The symbols which people devise to help cope with these limit situations become what we term religion. Thus sacred symbols deal with bafflement, pain and moral paradox by synthesising a people's worldview. Humankind always feels it has to make some sense out of the chaotic forces of life. Religion is that result expressing itself in sacred symbols.

In the article by Geertz, already cited, he defines religion more fully and then develops these points through the rest of the article. His extended definition of religion is that it is:

- a system of symbols which acts to
- establish powerful, pervasive and long-lasting moods and motivations in men, by
- formulating conceptions of a general order of existence
- clothing these conceptions with such an aura of factuality that
- the moods and motivations seem uniquely realistic.[76]

So with Geertz we have a religious system described as a cluster of sacred symbols woven into some sort of ordered whole. The meaning of the systems is stored in the symbols (be it a cross, crescent, roman collar or sacred book) which collectively give meaning to life as experienced by a given people at a given time. I will take up this concept of a cluster of symbols when I examine some such systems at work before and after Vatican II.

Haviland's definition of religion reflects Geertz's approach to religion as the answer to the human bafflement problem:

The beliefs and patterns of behaviour by which humans try to deal with what they view as important problems that cannot be solved through the application of known technology or techniques of organisation. To overcome these limitations people turn to the manipulation of supernatural beings or powers.[77]

We have looked at a variety of definitions or descriptions of religion from anthropologists. It seems to me that there are basically two poles to the approach. One pole is an explanation of religion from the phenomenological viewpoint and this is not an explanation so much as a record of observation while suspending judgment (the evolutionists). The other is a social approach arising out of the physical, social, ideological and psychological needs of human life, (the functionalists, structuralists and symbolists).

The second of these sees the social or psychological function of religion as one which attempts to:

- reduce anxiety
- provide comfort
- sanction human conduct
- enhance oral tradition through rituals
- foster social solidarity
- provide meaning through a system of symbols

We now have spent some time in examining questions of methodology in the study of religion, the various kinds of definitions of religion and illustrative examples, all of which places us in a good position to apply the insights from the first three chapters to Australian culture. Before we do that let us look at examples of religion in action in particular cultures.

Some examples of religion in cultures

Religion is part of all cultures. Sometimes it is not so easy to identify, but all cultures have the same needs to meet in terms of integrative demands. The Aborigines of Australia in the early days of white settlement were thought not to have had a religion. Indeed many cultures throughout the world do not have a word for 'religion'. The settlers used the European criteria of religion to assess whether the Aborigines had religion or not, like sacred rituals, ideas of God, religious stories, etc. They could not see any 'normal' signs of religion, no churches, no mention of God, no worship, so they presumed they had no religion. Today we hopefully know better. The integrative needs of the Aborigines were met in other holistic ways and to such an extent that we refer today to Aboriginal spirituality rather than Aboriginal religion to avoid the European connotations of what religion is.

In societies where religion is one strand or aspect of life, it can be either private or public. In Italy, to take a modern example, religion is public, it is part of public life. Beliefs about the Madonna lead to processions in public carrying statues of the Blessed Virgin Mary. The Feast of St Joseph is a public festival with special delicacies on sale. The imminent commencement of the ancient custom of Lent and repentance in preparation for the feast of Easter is announced by a public 'fling' in Italy (and Brazil, and elsewhere) with *Carnevale*.

In Australia, on the other hand, religion is, by and large, a private matter. There are no huge processions of statues through the streets and politicians do not in general mention God or religion in public speeches. The cultural matrix for white religion in Australia was

Anglo-Celtic culture, hence the reserve and private nature of Christianity by and large. Nevertheless religion is always there, even if partially hidden, ready to rise to the surface of public life.

Religion rising to the surface of public life

Expressions of religion in Australian culture

There are many expressions of religion in Australian culture. The 1991 census gives us the data for the following bar graphs. Figure 1 looks at Australia from the perspective of world religions while Figure 2 gives us the composition by denomination of Christianity in Australia. It should be noted here that often the word 'religion' is used rather loosely in Australia meaning a Christian denomination. The ABC Radio and Television make a point however of using the word more broadly, in the sense of primal, tribal and world religions as we shall see in chapter 6.

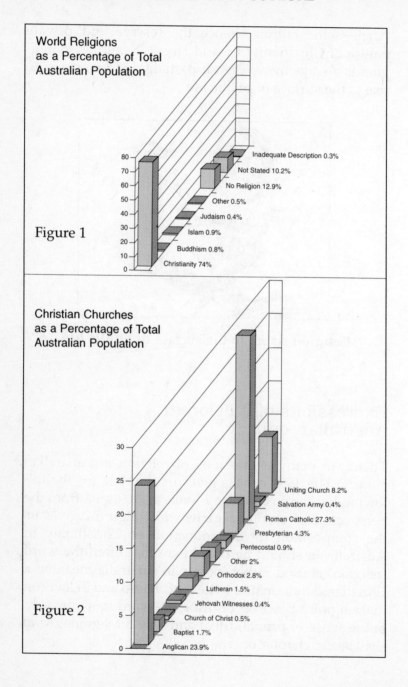

World Religions as a Percentage of Total Australian Population

Figure 1

Inadequate Description 0.3%
Not Stated 10.2%
No Religion 12.9%
Other 0.5%
Judaism 0.4%
Islam 0.9%
Buddhism 0.8%
Christianity 74%

Christian Churches as a Percentage of Total Australian Population

Figure 2

Uniting Church 8.2%
Salvation Army 0.4%
Roman Catholic 27.3%
Presbyterian 4.3%
Pentecostal 0.9%
Other 2%
Orthodox 2.8%
Lutheran 1.5%
Jehovah Witnesses 0.4%
Church of Christ 0.5%
Baptist 1.7%
Anglican 23.9%

Summary

We now are in a position to establish a framework for an understanding of culture and religion that we have gleaned from the first three chapters. We will use this framework which is eclectic by nature, for the remaining chapters.

Culture is the total way of life of a people including the artefacts, ideas, thought patterns and sign system of a people. The unilinear evolutionist theory of culture is rejected because from our experience of life we know that life does not evolve in a single progressive way. There are many ambiguities about progress. The usefulness of the needs theory is accepted and the view that sees culture as the product of the interaction of people with their physical, social and ideational environment, as well as the semiotic view that sees culture in terms of the interconnection of symbols giving meaning to life. Each theory has something to offer us in the understanding of culture and religion. It is not expected that one theory will be the best, or the only one, to explain all circumstances. The concepts, as defined above, of enculturation, acculturation, diffusionism, inculturation, symbiosis and socialisation and the host of terms used in connection with change are the tools to be used in the discussions of the following chapters.

Culture is seen also as relative rather than absolute, the elements of which are interconnected. Religion which is highly complex by nature, is a part of culture and so subject to the normal process of enculturation. Being a part of culture it too is dynamic and changes. But religion is also seen as polyvalent although the phenomenologist's and functionalist's (anthropologist's) understanding is often the one that is used in practice.

We conclude that the term 'religion' cannot be used univocally.

With this general conceptual framework, we now are in a position to apply it to the religious history of Australia (chapters 4 and 5) and the media (chapter 6), with a view to a deeper understanding of how religion operates from a cultural perspective.

Points to ponder:

1. Which of the above definitions of religion appeals to you? Explain your choice.

2. Do you think it is possible for a committed believer to study religion in an objective, non-confessional, phenomenological way? Explain your answer.

3. Give examples by way of evidence that religion is a private matter in Australian culture.

4. In what way do you see religion as a cultural system?

5. What inferences can you draw from the data in the bar graphs?

4

Imposing Anglo-Celtic culture

The method of this and the next chapter is to take the framework for culture and religion as outlined in the first three chapters and apply it to some aspects of the history of Australia. This will be done in a chronological way. Thus chapter 4 deals with the eighteenth century and chapter 5 with the nineteenth century.

The particular events and people chosen from history will tend to be those which are especially suited to anthropological interpretation. They are meant to be illustrative not exhaustive. Rather than take a given fixed cultural paradigm and apply it rigorously to events in history, I am doing it the other way round, that is, I will refer to specific events and people and then show how they illustrate some framework or aspect of anthropology. This is appropriate because history changes and some epochs illustrate a particular theory better than others. The headings of this and the next chapter illustrate this point. For example, it seems to me that one of the paradigms that one could apply to the eighteenth century is that of the imposition of Anglo-Celtic culture (acculturation) on the continent of Australia. It was the imposition of Anglo-Celtic culture on the Aborigines and on the emerging colony as it constructed its main institutions. The framework that goes with this is the unilinear theory of the progress of culture.

Aboriginal culture

The Aborigines were in Australia long before the whites arrived, before the Maoris or even the Morioris conquered New Zealand, before the European voyages of discovery in the fifteenth and sixteenth centuries, before even the Hebrews conquered the land of Canaan, before the ancient town of Jericho was founded or gold was discovered at Mycenae. As we saw, they were here more than fifty thousand years ago[78]. We are told that, in 1788, there were at least seven hundred and fifty five thousand Aborigines in Australia[79] spread over about six hundred language groups so that there would have been different cultures, or subcultures, rather than one uniform culture. Nevertheless we can make some general observations about what seems to have been common to all or most tribes.

The first thing to say is that the Aborigines would not have spoken about culture and religion as two separate entities. As with the Hebrews, what westerners call religion was part and parcel of life for the Aborigines. It was not compartmentalised. Religion was integrated into life. But the Europeans did not realise this at first. They knew nothing about the indigenous people. In fact the difference between the two cultures could hardly have been greater. The Aborigines were nomadic and content to live off the land, not asking for more than that. They were perhaps the most ancient of all peoples with a largely spiritual worldview encapsulated in their Dreaming. Their concepts of the world, person, egalitarianism, tribe, land and the stewardship of the land, possessions, ritual, work and time were distinctive. At the other end of the scale were the British, one of the most technically advanced people at the time, coming from the ideological background of the Renaissance, Reformation and the Enlightenment and from the technical background of the industrial revolution. One could hardly imagine two cultures further apart.

Dampier had called the Aborigines in northern Australia, the 'miserablest people in the world'. Aborigines were looked down upon and it is not surprising therefore that their evidence was not accepted in court - like women's testimony in ancient Israel. In the political sphere they were overlooked as well, not getting the vote until 1967.

Cook's view was more accurate, if expressed in somewhat faulty grammar:

> ...they may appear to some to be the most wretched people upon earth, but in reality they are far more happier than we Europeans; being wholly unacquainted not only with the superfluous but the necessary conveniences so much sought after in Europe. They are happy in not knowing the use of them. They live in tranquillity which is not disturb'd by the inequality of condition: The earth and the sea of their own accord furnishes them with all things necessary for life.[80]

I think Cook's description captures some of the striking characteristics of Aboriginal culture: their ability to live off the fruits of the earth in a simple lifestyle and their contentment with the necessities of life. Cook's description however must be seen against the background of nineteenth century Romanticism, of the concepts of 'Equality, Fraternity and Liberty', of the French Revolution and of the 'Noble Savage' ideology prevalent at the time. A certain willingness to fantasise about the conditions of all indigenous peoples 'discovered' in the eighteenth century and earlier, would have obscured the fact that for many Aborigines life was, to use an earlier phrase of the English philosopher Thomas Hobbes, 'solitary, poore, nasty, brutish and short'[81].

One also should not forget that the underlying anthropological theory, although more implicit than explicit, emanating from Europe through the Enlightenment would have been the unilinear evolutionist one of E.B. Tylor and Lewis Morgan which saw culture as progressing in a straight line from the lower to the higher; from savagery through barbarism to civilisation (cf. chapter 1 above). The Aborigines would have been at the bottom end of the straight line according to this theory. Hence the perceived need to 'civilise' them. An appreciation that all the white settlers, officials and missionaries were more or less influenced by this cultural outlook goes a long way to explaining their words and actions.

Having said that, we can ask: What was the attitude of missionaries in particular, as opposed to colonists, to Aborigines in the nineteenth century? Richard Watson, a Wesleyan leader had a very negative appreciation of Aborigines. He claimed that the Aborigine was:

> Without any knowledge of his Maker, ignorant of almost all useful arts; abandoned to gross and brutal passions when aroused; slothful and improvident when the impulse ceases; buried in dirt; ... thinking only, when thought is present, in the vainest and most puerile imaginations; oppressed with gloom, hearing an angry spirit in every breeze; gathering omens of ill from every meteor; without laws; herding together only on the principle which unites gregarious animals; without the comforts which the lowest degree of religious knowledge, when substantially true, supplies a life.[82]

Samuel Leigh thought Aborigines were 'barbarians' to whom had been assigned 'the lowest place in the scale of intellect'.[83] Samuel Marsden was another missionary who had a negative view of Aborigines. Although he tried initially to do something for them, he gradually, (says Breward), 'became convinced that they were not open to conversion and his interests as a landowner reinforced his support for the punitive policy against their resistance to the expansion of settlement'.[84]

Other opinions were more humane and Christian although often mixed with a biblical fundamentalism. C. Smith, a female missionary to the Boonandik of South Australia from 1845-1880, believed that 'Jesus Christ died to save this poor degraded son of Adam, that he indeed gave Himself a ransom for his soul'.[85] The Anglican Robert Cartwright, wrote that the Creator 'had made of one blood all the nations of the earth'.[86] The Rev Thomas Dove pointed out that some people view the Tasmanians as representative of the lowest form of human degradation, and *if* we look 'only' at their morality, it 'seems' as though they lack the quality of 'rational beings', *but if* we look at their skills in subsistence, hunting, etc, *then* in fact, the Aborigines display considerable mental ability.[87] The first person to be appointed to be a missionary specifically to the Aborigines in 1821, the Rev William Walker of the Wesleyan Missionary Society, took this typically evangelical theological approach: the Aborigines were descendants of Ham and under a curse. They were 'the progeny of him who was cursed to be a servant of servants to his brethren', but they were also 'about to stretch out their hands unto God'.[88]

In short the attitude of missionaries while more compassionate, reflects the paternalistic and sometimes racist attitudes of the ethnocentric culture from which they came. Not all reflected this attitude. Bishop Polding and Robert Cartwright in Australia and the Dominican, Las Casas, earlier in Latin America are outstanding examples of missionaries who most clearly saw the equality of all humankind before God - and were prepared to say so.

However the general negative attitude towards the indigenous people (Aborigines) would be true of other countries during the period of colonisation. Anthropology was not developed as a discipline. The whites thought the Aborigines had no religion, as David Collins said in 1798: traces of religion are to be found in all countries but, after intensive enquiry, he had to conclude that the Aborigines were an exception to this generalisation.[89] This conclusion followed a particular cultural understanding of religion, as we said above in chapter 3, that is, it presupposed certain manifestations of religion found in some cultures and generalised (incorrectly) from these.

But the Aborigines did have their Dreaming (or 'originating from Eternity'[90]). The knowledge of the stories about the creation of the world, the origin of human life, the spirit world, were all imparted to youngsters during initiation rites, and as they grew up, learning about life in general and how to survive. Malinowski refers to Andrew Lang's indication that belief in a tribal All-Father did exist among some Australian Aborigines.[91] This is possible but others like Swain think the All-Father belief is evidence of the influence of white culture.

The second thing to say is that the Aboriginal worldview is a sacramental one. That is they saw the material things of this world as pointing to other realities beyond the physical. The spirit world was present everywhere. Only a thin veil separated them. The things of this world reminded them of, and connected to, the spirit world. Some places were sacred sites, that is, had connections with the world of spirits.

One aspect that both the religious culture and the secular culture of the nineteenth century shared was its racism (in its crudest form: that there was a biologically-based superiority of white races over black) and the concomitant assumption that the great land of the South was largely *terra nullius*. One must distinguish here between the attitude of the Colonial Office and the settlers or graziers. The former were careful to distinguish between land that was uninhabited and that which was occupied, the latter not.

Reynolds has shown that even where the Colonial Office allowed crown land to be leased to graziers, it was on the condition that the Aborigines be allowed to continue to use the land for food, rituals, etc.[92] This often was disregarded by the graziers, particularly after the state governments were set up. Within that context, it can be said that the land grab went ahead and it has been only since the 1970s and with the 1993 Mabo High Court Case, that the painful national process of reconciliation and handing back some of the land is beginning. A parallel process in South Africa commenced with the first truly democratic General Elections of 1994, after three hundred years of colonial-type rule. In Canada and the USA the historical reality was that the indigenous peoples were often too small numerically and too powerless to give much weight to their claims.

White religion

Mary Kalantzis and others have pointed out that if one roughly divides up into blocks of fifty years the two hundred years of white settlement in Australia, one finds that the second block (1850-1900) is the one during which the foundational institutions of Australia were laid.[93] The period was one of strong British culture within a strong British Empire. It was prior to the migration waves of the next century, although there was Irish migration, and to a much smaller extent Chinese and American, due to the gold rush. It is this period that lays the foundations for all the myths about who Australians are. Many of these persist in the culture today.

But let us go back to the beginning with the arrival of the British with their religion in the late eighteenth and beginning of the nineteenth centuries. The religious scene was not a particularly edifying one. Governor Hunter in 1798, remarked, 'A more wicked, abandoned and irreligious people have never been brought together in any part of the world..', while T.W. Plummer in 1811, referred to the colony as 'little less than an extensive brothel'. Not much of an endorsement! However this view has been shown to be inaccurate or a distortion of reality by the work of the historian, Portia Robinson.[94] She has demonstrated by researching actual women (convicts and wives of convicts) of the times that the division of women into 'wives or concubines' (in Marsden's terms) is a gross distortion of the lives of women in the early part of the nineteenth century and that the first generation native-born children of ex-convicts had the normal range of values one would expect to find in any comparable society.

White religion (Christianity) was the official religion and, needless to say, worlds apart from Aboriginal religion. It was practised on a Sunday and by some (few) on other days of the week as well. The white conquerors brought a Christian religion called the 'Church of England' with them and this became the *de facto*, established religion in Australia (at least until the Church Act of 1836) which meant that the government supported it. Not all the whites agreed about religion so they built their own sacred sites like little houses. We probably will never know precisely what Aborigines would have said about this kind of religious practice in the eighteenth and nineteenth centuries, although some accounts that have come down to us comment at least indirectly.

One thing they did comment on was the white settler's hypocrisy. Outside the mission they noted the immorality of the white settler. Harris quotes an interesting case. They noted that missionaries preached to them a lot about sin and its consequences and thought that it could have been better directed at the white men. The white settler claims that he has a God of light. If he does why does he keep asking for the Aborigine's wife and daughters?:

> White fellow all about make a Light God ... What for white fellow always say you lend me yeener (woman) belonging to you, this night, so many nights, this moon ... then I give you bread, I give you milk, shirt ... when black fellow make a Light God then he never lend yeener to white fellow at all.[95]

The Aboriginal understanding of sharing the fruits of the earth led them to see the way the white missionaries doled out food as mean and miserly. Reynolds quotes the amusing case in North Queensland of some Aborigines when they had received some food and tobacco, asking rather pointedly: 'Does the One up in Heaven tell you to give us so little?'[96]

Right from the start with the interface of Christianity and Aboriginal culture the whites tried to make the blacks images of themselves in all aspects of their religion. The handing on process was one-way. There was certainly no question of religious inculturation, although, for example, L. Threlkeld's translation of Luke into the local Aboriginal language showed a sensitivity to the need to communicate in the language of the people being evangelised. Inculturation requires a two-way interaction as Azevedo mentioned above. In what was being done in the colony (and elsewhere in the world) there was only one-way traffic, that is, Christianity was being handed on. This was part of the general ethnocentric attitude, that is, that the whites were bringing a superior culture to the Aborigines. (The one-way handing on of a Eurocentric Christianity in fact continued for the next two hundred years. Only in recent decades has inculturation been taken seriously.)

And this was at the heart of the problem: civilisation and Christianity were inseparable in practice if not in theory. Many missionaries, having tried evangelisation first and got nowhere, decided that 'civilisation' should come first as a sort of pre-requisite to evangelisation. This was Marsden's early decision. Many simply became discouraged and said missionary work among the Aborigines was too difficult. Harris's book is full of such failed missionary endeavours which were often seen as a failure to civilise. Lord Stanley noting the failure of early missions described their work as 'the civilisation and protection of these people', and the Lutheran missionary, William Schmidt, commented on his missionary failures as failures to civilise.[97] This attitude persisted until much later. In 1972 the Democratic Labor Party Senator, J.A. Little opined:

Nobody who has fairly considered the history of this country could say that the Australian Aborigines, any more than the animal species of this disappearing continent before the white man came, would have survived through this generation, had it not been for the intervention of the white people, bringing the knowledge and the skills of Europe with them which enabled them to tackle the deteriorating environment of this country and make it what it is today.[98]

The Rev Richard Johnson like other high-minded members of the white community, adopted or fostered Aboriginal children as a means of bringing the Christian religion and civilisation to them. Marsden tried to 'civilise' his Aboriginal household boy but failed. Baptism of the children became a measure of civilisation. Unfortunately the willingness of missionaries to want to bring up Aboriginal children away from their parents ended up with the Aborigines taking flight or hiding their children whenever missionaries appeared.[99] John Harris has told the sad story of missionary work among the Aborigines in his tome, *One Blood*. Missionaries in general, not understanding the culture, complained about the wandering habits of the Aborigines. They wanted them to stay in one place and to teach them how to read and write, good manners, economic skills and appropriate gender-roles.

In Grimshaw's creative book, *Creating a Nation*, there is a very apt reference to this kind of forced acculturation that went on right from the earliest times. During Macquarie's time as governor he tried, in good faith, to make Europeans out of the Aborigines. The Black Native Institute was established in 1815 by William Shelley. In December 1816 Macquarie instituted a Congress of Aborigines at Parramatta:

The event initiated the visitors into the ways of British patriarchy. Aboriginal society had no individual leaders whose words were always to be obeyed; men and women both acted as leaders of different activities. Macquarie identified a prominent man within each language group, seated him upon a chair above the rest, and presented him with an engraved breastplate declaring him to be the chief of his tribe. Then the dozen Aboriginal children living and studying at the Native Institution arrived 'in a neat procession' with Mrs Macquarie and their teacher, Elizabeth Shelley. The boys were wearing tailored suits and caps, the girls linen bonnets and crisp white dresses. In the school the boys were taught gardening and the girls dressmaking. The Aboriginal women cried when they saw their children. The male chiefs were brought forward to 'examine the children's skills in the civilised habits of life', in this case their ability to recite the Christian catechism and to read aloud. One Aboriginal man reportedly exclaimed that his 'pickaninny would make a good settler'.[100]

Another example of forced acculturation is the case of Bennelong who was abducted forcibly in 1789 by Governor Phillip. The image of his living in the Governor's house, dressed in European clothes, taken to England in 1782 to be presented at court, would be humorous if not so tragically misguided. However it must be said that he came to like European food, clothes and alcohol and sadly ended his life in a state of being rejected by both the European and Aboriginal cultures.

Proselytism accompanied the attempts at 'civilisation'. Not that this was a primary objective but it became progressively more important in the colonies as time passed. When missionary work was attempted, it was not easy. They found the Aborigines more resistant to evangelisation than the South Pacific Islanders. The missionaries did not understand the Aborigines and certainly did not take Luzbetak's firm advice that the first thing to do is to observe the culture until one begins to see how it operates in life as regards primary, derived and integrative needs.

In the second half of the century, that well-known authority and author of Aboriginal culture, C.D. Rowley, seemed to think that the only way to succeed was to 'break the power and limit the influence of the old men, by disrupting the process of indigenous education which passed on the culture from old to young so that Christian teaching and literacy might replace them.'[101]

He was right in the sense that he had identified correctly one of the strongest means of enculturation, the formal and informal learning from elders. Remove that and the culture could die out and Christianity would have a chance of taking root. We know that in fact the Europeans did isolate the Aborigines on 'missions' and attempt to remove them from their elders, sometimes by sending the children to white foster-parents (especially in the twentieth century). Thus blows were struck at the very foundations of Aboriginal culture - severance of the enculturation processes followed by attempts at forced acculturation. As Eugene Stockton has pointed out, 'Aborigines differ from migrants in not having made a deliberate break with their culture'.[102] It was forced on them.

Attempts at Acculturation:
John Diremera and Francis Conaci,
two of Salvado's[103] Aboriginal Catholics

The culture that was imposed in the nineteenth century did have some latent religious element. True enough, the convicts generally were not religiously inclined as we saw above, except for some Irish and Scots who were more likely to have had religious training, according to Grocott and therefore more likely to participate in their respective churches. He sums it up as follows: 'Overall it is hard to escape the conclusion that only a small percentage of transported convicts had any genuine interest in religious observance and beliefs'[104]. It was however, the free settlers such as the Scottish Presbyterians, people like John Dunmore Lang, and Catholics like Caroline Chisholm (English), and Mary MacKillop (Australian born of Scottish background) who brought a strong tradition of religious belief and commitment to the colony. The women were often the faith nurturers in the difficult environment of NSW in the early nineteenth century. Charlotte Waring who came to Australia in 1826, married the following year and wrote a children's book entitled, *A Mother's Offering to Her Children.* The kind of trust in Providence that must have carried people like her through life is described:

Teach us to quit this transitory scene,
With decent triumph and a look serene;
Teach us to fix our ardent hopes on high,
And having lived to God, in him to die.[105]

So much for the kind of culture that was present and imposed on the Aborigines in many cases, and even on the settlers in more indirect ways. Let us now look at the more formal structures that quickly grew out of this culture.

Setting up church structures

The setting up of church structures falls neatly into the general pattern of establishing institutions in society at large in the second part of the nineteenth century. On the political front, responsible government was granted to NSW and Victoria in 1855, South Australia and Tasmania in 1856, Queensland in 1859, and Western Australia in 1890. In time this developed into the Federation of 1901. On the judicial front the whole legal systeme also was set up along the lines of English law.

As regards education, the schools were set up parallel to English government schools though there were Scottish and Irish influences. Universities were founded in the capital cities: Sydney (1852), Melbourne (1854), Adelaide (1874), Hobart (1890), Brisbane (1909) and Perth (1911). Other institutions such as museums, art galleries and libraries were established also. All these institutions were modelled more or less on what the settlers knew best, the British system. The whole process and cultural background is symbolised in the architecture of Sydney University, the oldest of the Australian universities.

It is not surprising that the churches also moved to set up structures during this time. The first Anglican bishop was William Grant Broughton who arrived in 1829 as an archdeacon, but was installed as bishop in 1836. Tasmania became a diocese in 1842 and Sydney the archdiocese in 1847 with Melbourne and Adelaide becoming dioceses in the same year.

In the Catholic Church the hierarchy also was set up. John Bede Polding was, of course, the first Catholic bishop of Sydney in 1836, but the hierarchy was not established until 1842 with the Archbishop in Sydney and, in rapid succession, bishops in Hobart (1842), Adelaide (1844), Perth (1845), Melbourne (1848) and Brisbane (1859), as well as others in the country areas. It proved to be Irish and Roman-trained, although the first Catholic bishop in Australia was ironically, an English Benedictine.

The other churches also set up their structures during this period adding to the diversity, richness and complexity of the religious culture in Australia. Rev John Dunmore Lang arrived for the Presbyterians in 1823. For the Methodists there was Rev Samuel Leigh in 1812. The smaller denominations arrived somewhat later: the Congregationalists in 1799, the Baptists in 1831, the Christadelphians in 1877, the Plymouth Brethren, Mormons, and Seventh-Day Adventists in the 1880s.[106]

Church buildings grace most Australian towns and villages. In the larger Australian towns, even today, one sees around the central square or park area, the four major Christian denominations announced by their churches, the Anglican, Catholic, Methodist or Wesleyan and Presbyterian Churches. Frequently the former Presbyterian or Methodist Church building is now the Uniting Church in Australia (hereafter the UCA). The old wooden church on the hilltop in small outback towns is a noticeable feature and legacy of Australia's religious origins.

The impact of Christianity is evident also in the educational system dating from the earliest times since white settlement. Church schools sprang up with the Catholics now providing schooling for about a quarter of the Australian population. In the nineteenth century the religious orders of men and women were recruited to Australia to staff the Catholic schools. Other traditions of church schools arose too with Anglican, Presbyterian, Methodist schools. In the welfare area, many churches set up hospitals, clinics and old age homes. These are the institutions that we still have with us today and are living testimonials to the influence of Christianity on Australian society.

All this setting up of church structures was helping to give shape to the subcultures that each church group represented.

Irish Catholicism

A substantial part of the white Christian religion was Irish Catholicism. This was due not so much to the number of Irish convicts (most were from England and Scotland) but from the immigration wave in the 1840s after the depression and potato crop failures in Ireland. The economic scene in Australia however was not much better. The following statistics[107] illustrate the surge in the numbers of Irish during the 1840s:

Year	Anglican	Catholic
1836	54,621	21,898
1851	93,137	56,899
Increase	41%	141%

But right from the start of the colony they formed a group. Without a resident priest they nurtured their faith in Sydney around the homes of the stonemason, James Dempsey (Kent Street) and William Davis, near the present church of St Patrick's near Circular Quay. When the first priest was appointed in 1820 they were already well-organised. This organisation was their response to the derived needs of the group as they formed a distinct subculture in the colony. The Vinegar Hill uprising in 1804[108] was one clear, if unfortunate manifestation of this vibrant subculture.

Their brand of Catholicism was very Irish in the way they practised their religion. The attendance patterns at Mass and Benediction, the prayerbooks, the rosary beads, the devotion to the Sacred Heart and to Mary, the prayers of petitions for all and sundry, novenas, and the wearing of scapulars, regular auricular confessions, the invocations of special saints like Patrick, Joseph and Finbarr, great veneration for and loyalty to the Pope, and placing priests and religious on a pedestal - all these made up the whole thing called Irish Catholic practices, or 'the faith'.

The placing of priests on a religious pedestal is an interesting point. The anthropologist, Malinowski, in the context of discussing religion, science and magic, believed that myth enforced belief and that the magicians who helped enforce the beliefs and practised the magic were generally, in primal societies, the bright, intelligent ones in the tribe.[109] There is certainly a whole religious myth surrounding the priesthood in Catholicism. A history of the priesthood shows that from no mention at all of priests in the New Testament, it slowly evolved and increased in importance until we have the Medieval/Tridentine priesthood with a very elaborate theology.

Ordination almost turned the candidate into a kind of superman. This was, in Geertz's terminology, a central symbol to the religious culture of many Catholics.

After Trent the difference of priests (in contradistinction to the Reformers and their emphasis on the priesthood of all believers) was further underlined by the new training of priests which was six or seven years in seminaries in isolation from the rest of the population. The doctrine of papal infallibility in the nineteenth century reinforced the hierarchical nature of Catholicism. The priests benefited from this move, as they were in some way, according to a particular ecclesiology, the representatives of the bishop who was the representative of the pope.

In medieval times the priests tended to be those who had some education, those who could read and write, and thus added to their growing collection of powers. They could read and write, forgive sin, they had the power to change the bread and wine into the body and blood of Christ, they had the power to build churches, to refuse people a Christian marriage ceremony or burial, etc. They were very prominent public persons in the villages and cities of Europe and still are in some places even today. The laity gave them powers by collusion. They asked whether they could receive communion (in the days prior to Vatican II) after having eaten something absentmindedly, they asked them to pray for their dead. They asked for all kinds of permission and help including financial and personal matters. So that in short, the model of priesthood made the priest a powerful person.

The Irish Catholics in Australia inherited this view of priests and let us not forget that illiteracy was greatest among the Irish.[110] The pedestal on which they placed him might well have been higher than some other cultures. Grocott's opinion is that Catholic convicts were more 'susceptible to their priests' than Protestants[111]. He had all these powers, and in some uneducated eyes was close to a magician. (Vatican II and its aftermath changed this cultural perception of priesthood. I will return to this issue in chapter 5 when I analyse the religious acculturation phenomenon known to Christians as Vatican II.)

These practices left their mark on Australian Catholicism. It was not only the Irish in Australia who followed these patterns but it influenced the whole Catholic Church in Australia to the extent that one could characterise it by saying it was Irish Catholicism. This needs to be qualified as I will do below, nevertheless a process of religious acculturation went on. Even today, there are, within the same church, sectional persistence of older religious customs - pockets of people who favour devotion to the rosary, Marian devotions in the month of May, the use of miraculous medals, - all these in spite of the religious turmoil which accompanied Vatican II.

One may wonder what people outside Irish Catholicism thought of it. What did the English think of the Irish? According to Molony, they 'assumed the Irish were priest-ridden, superstitious, anti-intellectual and indolent. In Australia the Irish not only caused irritation by their popery, but also by the fact that they showed faint yet clear signs of wanting to rise in social status from the level of the bog to that of the professional, merchant and propertied classes, and even into the higher realms of the Establishment preserve, government itself.'[112] There was not much empathetic understanding of other people's religious culture in those days!

For the Catholics it was a question of maintaining their identity as a minority in the face of Protestantism. Not surprisingly Catholicism formed itself into a ghetto - own schools, churches, clubs, scouts, football teams, bushwalking clubs. Many Australian towns have a 'Vatican Hill' or 'Vatican block', a church, presbytery, primary school and convent. All of these issues are of interest because, anthropologically speaking, they are expressions of a group (Catholics) meeting their derived needs. Other churches did much the same thing depending on their size and resources.

The Presbyterians or Scots in 1802, under the leadership of James Mein, did arguably much the same in taking themselves off to Portland Head on the banks of the Hawkesbury (outside Sydney) and starting a Presbyterian community there with a church called Ebenezer which doubled as a school. The German Lutherans in South Australia are another example. They had been forced in Prussia to unite with the Reformed Church in one national church. When they were offered land in South Australia in the 1830s, they were overjoyed because this was a way they could maintain their religious culture and identity. Their settlement at Hahndorf near Adelaide is a witness to this culture even today.

In all these withdrawals the place of schools plays an important part because of its centrality to the enculturation process. It becomes the standard-bearer in the campaign for self-preservation.

Schools and mixed marriages

Let me return to the Catholic schools situation which is illustrative of what many denominations were doing. Firstly let me say that there was much encouragement from Rome to set up Catholic schools. Fully state-controlled and purely secular schools had been formally condemned in 1864 by Pius IX in his comprehensive *Syllabus of Errors*. The Australian bishops cited this document at their Council meeting in 1869. Education, they said, must be infused by a religious atmosphere. In 1879 the bishops of New South Wales issued a Joint Pastoral Letter condemning secular schools as being, among other things, 'seedplots of future immorality, infidelity and lawlessness ... '[113]

In attempting to meet derived needs through the establishment of church schools, the curriculum was seen as vital. No curriculum is politically innocent. When the Catholics secured their schools they introduced a strong Irish cultural flavour through the saints, feast days, prayers and hymns of the religious education syllabus in particular and through the informal curriculum in general, to counteract the British imperial culture found in other (government) schools. Schooling for the churches was to be an important part of the enculturation process.

Other than the Irish-Catholics another group that lays great store by schools is the Jewish community. Not only in the past, but currently, the Jewish place for learning, the Yeshivas, are critical to the avoidance of assimilation and the maintenance of a Jewish identity in the galuth (the world at large). They maintain these schools in spite of enormous financial strain on the Jewish community.[114] Fundamentalist Christian schools are another example.

So-called 'mixed marriages' (marriages between Catholics and Protestants) were likewise rejected and frowned upon as threatening the ghetto mentality of the persecuted. The theme is an old one. In the Old Testament, after the Babylonian exile some of the prophets preached against marriage with aliens as a threat to the culture (Ezra 10:3; Nehemiah 13:23-25; Malachi 2:10-16). The hatred of the Jews for the Samaritans was a constant object lesson in what happens if one intermarries and contaminates the 'religious' gene pool. Australian Catholics thought in this way, if not exactly in these words.

When the Irish bishops arrived in the 1860s they were appalled to find so many mixed marriages.[115] Marrying someone from one's own religious group was seen as essential to the preservation of the religious subculture. That and Catholic schooling were the cornerstones of the Catholic subculture. Remove them and one's culture might go.

The state/religion relationship

There was a close if difficult relationship between state and religion right from the beginning of white settlement. The state initially saw religion as a given, as part of the British culture. Anglicanism came with settlement. It was the *de facto* state religion for a while. However it was soon evident that other denominations were not happy with the privileged treatment of

Anglicanism. Neither was Governor Bourke as we shall see shortly.

The fact is that the Anglican Church was the *de facto* state religion, and thus the Head of State (Governor) in NSW was effectively the head of the church prior to the 1836 Church Act. An incident that illustrates this concerns Marsden. He had rejected a request of the governor to read some secular government notices at the end of service. Macquarie, however, exerted his authority and insisted that he do so. The governor prevailed. The fact that Macquarie was paying his salary probably also persuaded Marsden to back down.

However, it was Governor Bourke who introduced the Church Act of 1836. Up to this stage Anglicans had received privileged treatment - ministers had their salaries paid and funds were available for church buildings and schools. The 1836 Church Act provided for equitable division of public funds for the support of the principal religious denominations. Bourke was opposed to an Anglican monopoly of funds, not on religious grounds, but because he felt all religious bodies required encouragement to enable them to contribute to the well-being of the colony. Until its repeal in 1862 Catholics and other denominations were delighted with this equality of government recognition. They saw the Act, as O'Farrell points out, as the Magna Carta of their religious liberty[116] which saw to it that all were treated equally.

Culturally, the 1836 Church Act was a big shift - Bourke was saying that he recognised the equality of the different denominations before the state. It fore-shadowed the distancing of government from religion in Australia, yet without ceasing to support all expressions of it. However, this relationship underwent a bumpy ride for the next hundred years and more, as aid to church schools was firstly withdrawn in the 1870s and 1880s, and then reintroduced in the 1960s. None of these moves occurred without much debate and acrimony.

The withdrawal of financial aid to church schools needs comment. Let me expand on this. This move of withdrawing financial aid strangely was not seen as detrimental to religion as it ensured that all religions were treated equally. It removed one source of dissension among churches as they could not agree on a national system of education. In the 1860s leading advocates of national education, of all denominations, wanted to keep religion (broadly conceived) in the curriculum as it provided an orientation to the broad principles of religion and morality.

By helping the churches and their schools financially the government was promoting education. By the 1840s many people in and out of government were seeing education as providing a major contribution to social reform rather than religion. Education would help to civilise, refine and inculcate manners. It was seen as part of the culture to be transmitted.

Aid to churches by way of paying salaries was withdrawn also over time and before the withdrawal of aid to the church schools. This occurred in South Australia in 1851, followed by NSW in 1862 and Victoria in 1872. This was not, according to Hogan, the separation of church and state as in the USA, because in many ways religion continued to enjoy favoured treatment by the state, as we saw above. In recent times, Corkhill makes this point in relation to the federal government letting the churches off the hook in terms of the Sex Discrimination Act of 1993.

Another reason why the state was prepared to help the churches and one that loomed large in the early days of the colony, was the utility one: religion could play the role of the moral policeman. In other words 'religion' was being defined in functional terms.

The instructions which accompanied the 1787 Commission given to Arthur Phillip, as Hogan points out, stated that the first governor was to 'enforce a due observance of religion and good order among the inhabitants of the new settlement, and that you do take such steps for the due celebration of public worship as circumstances will permit.'[117] It can be mentioned in passing that the Protestant churches in particular played precisely this role in trying to curb the drinking and gambling problem in Australia at the end of the nineteenth century.

Some individuals also took on this role of moral reformers but for different reasons. Some examples of women in the colony will help to remind us of the largely unsung role of women in history in general. Bessie Harrison Lee is one example. She was a notable writer and speaker in Melbourne who joined the Young Women's Christian Temperance Union[118] and in time became their president. She had experienced the bitter side of alcoholism at the hands of an uncle and aunt and hence campaigned with conviction for temperance. Another woman of note was Louisa Lawson, born in 1848 near Mudgee, NSW, and who was editor of the women's journal *Dawn*. In their own way each of these women did much to promote better treatment of women through the promotion of women's civil liberties.

Other women, such as the wife of the Anglican Archbishop of Melbourne, Mrs Frances Perry, cross-examined women who wanted to enter the Lying-in

Hospital (later the Royal Women's Hospital) as to the parentage of the unborn baby. Failure to do so might result in not being admitted to the hospital; some unmarried mothers borrowed certificates in their need! The churches always advocated marriage, and early marriage in particular as a way to avoid promiscuity and keep venereal disease as contained as possible.

Later in the nineteenth century the Catholics had cause to reflect on church/state relationships in the wake of the unification of Italy and the gradual loss of the Papal States. The Catholic Church became quite disillusioned with the State. This was probably in their minds when, in Sydney, the *Freeman Journal* cautioned that the Anglicans should learn 'to decline State patronage for their religion as its most dangerous and deadly enemy'.[119]

Women and religion

The role of women in the determination of culture, and religious culture in particular, has been obfuscated successfully in most accounts of history. It is only now that histories are beginning to be rewritten with greater sensitivity to women. On more general issues of social justice, it is interesting to note that in the 1880s it was women who played a prominent part in placing all kinds of awkward questions on the political and industrial agenda, such as whether a man's wages should cover his wife and children as well; whether women were being exploited in the workforce and what wages women should be paid.[120] The Young Women's Christian Temperance Union, mentioned above, by the beginning of the twentieth century succeeded in persuading many Protestant churches to replace the wine used at the Lord's Supper with grape juice in their services.

About this time the free thinker Harriet Dugdale of Melbourne was not slow in suggesting that the dominance of men over women was one of the outcomes of organised religion. The movement to liberalise the divorce laws was another instance where women (and some men) were trying to get things changed because the laws as they stood were disadvantageous to women (and as Muslims are doing today in Australia, as we will see in chapter 5). Sadly not all the churches were attuned to what was being said. The Presbyterians, however, did support the divorce law reform in the 1880s and 1890s.

In many ways, in a patriarchal society, it took outstanding people like Blessed Mary MacKillop, the Sisters of Charity and Caroline Chisholm to go against the tide and remind society of the contribution of women:

> For all the clergy you can dispatch, all the schoolmasters you can support, all the churches you can build, and all the books you can export, you will never do much good, without what a gentleman in that Colony very appropriately called 'God's police' - wives and little children - good and virtuous women.[121]

Chisholm was criticised often because she assumed that all women needed the protection of a home and a husband; that women should be placed in jobs where they would have a reasonable chance of being well married; that women's wages should be kept on a lower scale than men's because higher wages would tempt girls to remain single and encourage men to be lazy and rely on their wives' industry. All this would upset the design of nature. What Chisholm believed, however, was the cultural view of the time and it is invalid to retroject today's insights into the past.

In many ways Chisholm dared to be countercultural. Her agenda was not the agenda of the administrators or patriarchy as they would say now. She raised issues like the over-crowding and poor hygiene in the cities; abandoned wives and children during the gold rush; wives overworked because husbands were out drinking; domestic servants exploited. Chisholm suggested opening up squatters' leased lands to free selection for smallholdings. She also brought about the much-needed revision of shipping regulations.

> The churches encouraged women to marry and so rein in the men and produce children, and eventually productive citizens, for the colony. Clergymen saw women as more spiritual than men and less rational because of their child-bearing ability.

Another example of the leadership role women did play was that of Mother Janet Lancaster in Melbourne. Originally a Methodist, she founded the Good News Hall, a Pentecostal-style church in North Melbourne in 1909.[122] On the intellectual side of religion, Breward quotes Mrs Emily Herman, a Sydney Presbyterian minister's wife, who wrote books 'on the philosophy of religion and prayer as well as reviewing books for the *Australian Christian World*'.[123]

Some Anglican and Protestant women in the 1880s and 1890s were pushing for the recognition of women in the churches as reported in the Melbourne Church of England, *Messenger*. They were promoting the vote of women in parish and synod elections and called for the revival of the ancient order of deaconesses. It bore some fruit in that the Sydney Anglican diocese had appointed Mary Schleicher as a deaconess in 1886 and her sister, Selma, in 1889.[124] By the turn of the century there were nine deaconesses but their work was ill-paid and carried little social status; there were also sisterhoods and nuns. The Presbyterian and Methodist Churches also had deaconesses. Sr Laura Francis was a successful Methodist travelling evangelist at the beginning of the twentieth century.[125] Needless to say, the question of the role of women in the churches has not disappeared.

In 1904, at the Australian Catholic Congress in Melbourne, Miss Annie Golding of Sydney had prepared a paper on the case for giving the vote to women basing it on a biblical foundation in Genesis. Her paper was presented - but by a priest! Protestants were divided. Many male and female supported the female vote; others opposed it. Catholic Archbishop John O'Reilly said it 'unsexes and vulgarises'.[126] The domestic role of women was stressed as divinely instituted.

What we see in the above is the phenomenon of change from within by a group of women and some men who were trying to change the patriarchal or kyriarchal[127] culture from within. The successes of this movement were neither immediate nor complete, but it began something and it did register some advances, such as the vote and the ordination of women in some denominations.

Imported sectarianism

Religion was mainly Christian, eurocentric and sectarian in the nineteenth century in Australia. As such, it reflected the religion of the countries from which the people came. It had a strong influence on the culture as is seen in most countries with a Christian basis. Sunday is a day of worship, public holidays like Good Friday and Christmas are observed; morality is assumed to be along the Judeo-Christian lines of the ten commandments and (sometimes) along the lines of Christian charity. (Some liberals were not slow in pointing out the contradictions between Christian preaching about love and Christian praxis, as the Aborigines had done earlier).

Unfortunately, Christians were far from living in peace with each other. The sectarian nature of religion in Australian culture is well described by Edmund Campion in his book about growing up as Catholics in Australia, entitled, *Rockchoppers*. Australian religious history starts off on a very un-ecumenical note, as indeed did the conquest of the Indies by the Catholic Spanish and Portuguese conquistadors. Governor Phillip on 3 February, 1788, took his oath of office which included the following statement against popery: 'I Arthur Phillip, do declare that I do believe that there is not any Transubstantiation in the Sacrament of the Lord's Supper or in the Elements of Bread and Wine at or after the Consecration thereof by any Person whatsoever ...'[128]

Campion describes the general atmosphere in the nineteenth century created among Catholics by the reign of the conservative Pius IX and his stand against the liberalism that was sweeping Europe at the time, in particular his reaction to the revolutions of 1848. Added to this *angst* was the gradual losing of the Papal States. The 1864 *Syllabus of Errors* itemised all that was wrong with society at the time according to the pope and gave Catholics (and Australian bishops in particular) the official party line to pursue. This was followed up in 1870 with the doctrine of papal infallibility which concentrated the inward-looking focus of Catholicism even more on the pope who was regarded by some as 'owning' the church. There was only one true church for Catholics and other churches were not to be encouraged. The few liberal Catholics of the time, Acton, Newman and Montalembert made no impact on the direction Catholicism was moving.

Campion describes the Australian reaction to this as follows:

> This sore nerve was one of the reasons why Catholics in Australia created their own subculture. Although they were intensely Australian, indeed one of the main creative forces of Australian nationalism, on this one point of religious liberty they were unsure of where they stood as Catholics. So they created for themselves a sort of Ghetto. Today the Sydney telephone book lists survivals of the ghetto mentality: the Catholic Bushwalking Club, The Catholic Business Service, the Catholic Club for Seafarers.... there is even a Catholic organisation for homosexuals....[129]

There was a corresponding Protestant side to the sectarianism. The Australian Protestant Defence Association (APDA) was founded in 1901. One of its aims was to counter the undue Catholic influence on the government of the day. Where Protestants were always loyal to the British Crown, flag and anthem, Australian Catholics became more nationalistic and were inclined to run the Australian flag up their flagpoles and sing, *Advance Australia Fair*. This attitude was fuelled by Archbishop Mannix[130] with great skill. Empire Day became Australia Day as they turned to Mary Help of Christians, patroness of Australia.

Among the more colourful anti-Roman books were the writings of T.E. Ruth. The titles say it all: *Is the Papacy Anti-British?*, *Rome Rule in Australia*, *The Real Issue: Pope or King?*, and *Dr Mannix as Political Commander-in-Chief of a Sordid Trade War*. Articles by Herbert Brookes (son-in-law of Alfred Deakin) in *The*

Vigilant were also in the same vein. Later this century, between 1945-1979, a newspaper called *The Rock*, started by Wallace Campbell, carried on the anti-Catholic bigotry with a circulation of about thirty thousand in its heyday.

The most compelling reason for Protestants to be anti-Catholic was that Catholics were seen to be un-Christian in their teachings and practices. They did not support the Protestants in their efforts on Sabbatarianism and opposition to drinking and gambling. Canon D.B. Knox, Principal of Moore College in Sydney, on radio in 1969 discussing the issue of state aid to Catholic schools referred to the 'superstitious teachings' which contradict the Christian gospel.[131]

Sectarianism:
cartoon from
The Rock

John Dunmore Lang was another individual who fuelled the sectarianism during the nineteenth century. He was a Scottish minister, self-righteous moralist, writer, newspaper publisher, republican, gaolbird and radical politician. He came to Australia in 1823 and reacted strongly to Caroline Chisholm's project of promoting immigrants who were Catholic. (On the other hand he helped her privately and supported the civil rights of Catholics.) This he saw as a popish plot to 'Romanise the Australian colonies'. Similar arguments were used often in South Africa by Calvinists (Presbyterians) against the government when (white) immigrants from 'Catholic' countries, like Portugal and Italy were being allowed into the country.

Lang's extreme language against Catholics was immortalised in his pamphlet, *Popery in Australia and the Southern Hemisphere; and how to check it effectively*. The *Sydney Morning Herald* (hereafter *SMH*) thought it 'noticeable for its impartiality; it abuses everybody' and thought it written in bad taste and likely to disgust everyone.[132] Indicative of the time and attitudes, Lang and Polding never met each other during their lives in Sydney. Lang finally visited him when Polding was on his deathbed.

The Methodist attitude to Catholicism was no different. They saw the evil of Catholicism as embodied in the pope. *The Christian Advocate* put it like this:

> We believe that Popery is the greatest evil, as well as the social and religious enemy of mankind, that the world has ever seen, and that it is so because it is a *false religion* - a huge and complicated system of blasphemy and superstition.[133]

People like Chisholm, Ullathorne, and Lang, however, were united against transportation. The misery of those transported were helped by many religious people. The Sisters of Charity who helped the women in the Parramatta female factory, as it was known, is one example.

As regards Catholicism there was a subtle change in its orientation during the nineteenth century. In terms of cultural anthropology, the Catholic Church turned through a process of diffusion, if not acculturation, from a very Irish Catholic Church to a more Roman-type Church. Some would see this distinction as invalid, in that many saw the two aspects as complementary. But the point I am making is that made by Molony about the administration in the Catholic Church.[134] The catalysts in this process were the bishops trained in Rome during the time of Pius IX. Australia was not the only country, though, where Catholicism became more Roman during the highly authoritarian period from Pius IX to Pius XII.

It was a period of little or no *inculturation*. All Christian churches tried to teach Christianity by foisting on the Aborigines a European brand of Christianity. There was no interaction between Christianity and the culture or cultures. In fact the idea of inculturation was not promoted until very recently and most of the twentieth century repeated the mistakes of the nineteenth. (One of the classical examples of inculturation today is the use of the Aboriginal smoking ceremony as part of the rite of forgiveness in the Catholic Eucharistic celebration. It was used in the beatification ceremony for Mary MacKillop, but ironically, for the majority [whites] of the people present at Randwick Racecourse, it would have been fairly meaningless, since they have no smoking ceremony in their culture).

What happened in the schools could be interpreted by recourse to Schermerhorn's theoretical framework, cell D (cf.p.159). The State had centripetal goals (assimilation of the schools in one system) whereas the individual denominations had centrifugal goals (not wanting to integrate) and therefore conflict resulted.

The divisiveness of denominationalism in the nineteenth century was a scandal to society. The fruits of the Christian faith in its various forms seem to be self-interest and competition.

Among the nineteenth century liberals who were the intellectual offspring of the Enlightenment, there was the full range of positions from true believers through deists and agnostics to atheists. Some objected to religion, others promoted tolerance.

Summary

In this chapter we have reviewed the largely unsuccessful imposition of Anglo-Celtic culture on the Aboriginal tribes of Australia. The Aborigines were initially despised by many discoverers such as Dampier, although others, such as Cook, had a more sympathetic assessment of the Aborigines, even if coloured by nineteenth century romanticism. Missionaries did not, in general, have a very high regard for Aborigines and some thought they had no religion at all. They wanted to civilise them first and then make Anglo-Celtic Christians out of them. In many ways it was forced acculturation. Proselytism went hand in hand with attempts at enforced 'civilisation'. The removal of Aboriginal children from their families in order to 'civilise' them was one action which damaged Aboriginal culture the most since it destroyed the link of handing down the culture from elders to the younger generations.

The British culture was not able to impose itself on Irish Catholicism. Their culture was strong and they rejected any initial attempts to destroy or even dilute it. The Mannix era typified this. They reinforced their own culture by developing structures which preserved their cultural identity, especially schools and the principle of marrying within the tribe, as in fact did the Scottish Presbyterians and the Methodists. However, with time and better education, the Irish culture did accept many aspects of the British culture as what was originally British, Irish or Scottish, melted into what was becoming Australian. Towards the end of the nineteenth century there was a curious process of acculturation whereby Irish Catholicism in Australia was fast becoming Catholicism in the Roman mould - a point alluded to in this chapter and which will develop in the next chapter.

The Anglo and Irish cultures both succeeded in suppressing the role of women in society and therefore in the colony. That was simply the nature of European culture at the time. Only now in the twentieth century is history being rewritten so as to do justice to the achievements of women.

In this chapter we noted also that sectarianism was one aspect of Anglo-Celtic culture that was handed down in the society together with the rest of the cultural baggage that was passed on. There were some notable exceptions to sectarianism on both the Protestant and Catholic sides.

Points to ponder:

1. If the Catholic identity in Australia needed so many institutions, why did they never found a Roman Catholic political party?

2. To what extent is the Catholic Church in Australia still Irish or Roman today?

3. Would you still see Catholicism and Protestantism as subcultures? Give reasons for your opinion.

4. Will the disappearance of sectarianism lead to loss of identity for religious subcultures, or vice versa?

5. What is the ideal state/religion relationship in your opinion? Why?

6. How might the religious scene in Australia have developed had Christians agreed to having only one system of schools (a government system) in the nineteenth century?

5

Change, acculturation and persistence in the twentieth century

Not all people handle change well. I recall that years ago our congregation was looking for more people to read at the Sunday worship. I strongly advocated the button-hole method as the best for results. This meant approaching talented people personally and inviting them to do a certain job. Fired by this theory I approached a husband-and-wife couple whom I had noticed attending for many months thinking that I had two certain takers in my sights. When I put my request to them the reply was not what I expected. The couple was thinking of leaving the church because they had had enough of all the changes in the service, all the bobbing up and down, the singing and responding, and kiss of peace, etc.! So much for the changes introduced by Vatican II!

In this century, there certainly have been many challenging changes. If one looks across the century there are a number of examples one could pick out as typical of the diffusion, persistence and even acculturation that occurred in the religious culture, or subcultures, in Australia. This will be my agenda in this chapter. I hope that these illustrations will provide a deeper insight into the way religion operates in everyday life, at least from the anthropological angle.

Let me start with that famous cultural icon, Daniel Mannix.[135] My aim is not to rehash an already over-worked historical figure but to gain some cultural insights into what Mannix did and said, wearing anthropological spectacles.

Mannix: challenging the culture

Mannix was one person who, both consciously and unconsciously, sought to bring about change. He was indeed an agent of 'diffusion' as described in chapter 2 and in the language of semiotics, a symbol of Irish Catholicism. He carefully exploited a number of aspects of Australian society. As an Irishman with a strong sense of nationalism, he was able to address the issue of the disadvantaged socio-economic condition of the Irish ('uplifting the working class').[136] As he said in an address to a congregation in Clifton Hill, Melbourne, on 12 November, 1915: Catholics would not be 'the hewers of wood and the drawers of water in this State' and despite the difficulty of promotion Catholics must aim for 'the highest position in the land'.[137]

As archbishop he had the political influence and opportunity to make public statements diffusing ideas or provoking change in the community. Politically he was able to push the 'No-vote' in the conscription issue (in opposition to other church leaders), claim rights for Catholics, and express an opinion on Ireland contrary to the prevailing government view. A bit surprisingly for those times, and given his background and role as a Catholic bishop, he championed a wider role for women in public affairs and expressed the hope that more scholarships would be made available for women to study at university.[138] In this sense he was countercultural within his own church, but not within his Irishness.

Not surprisingly, Mannix was warned by the Vatican both through the Apostolic Delegate and later by a letter from the Sacred Congregation of Propaganda in 1918, about his outspokenness on the war issue, conscription, and the Irish question.[139] He was not conforming to the accepted religious (Vatican) culture of doing things; he was presenting the 'wrong' symbol of Catholicism as far as the Vatican was concerned; he did not cooperate with the 'Roman mould' plan. However, although he upset the Vatican, his actions reenforced the Irish/Catholic subculture. In this way he was ambivalent. Because he did not go along with the other Catholic bishops he was threatening the handing down of the tradition (the process of socialisation) that said the bishops should agree and present a united front to the rest of the world. On the other hand he was exploiting anti-British feeling through the conscription issue, thus uniting the Irish Catholics behind him (and in this way consolidating the socialisation process for Catholics). It must be said that the Irish uprising of 1916 was seized on by Britain supporters in Australia who questioned Irish loyalty in Australia and thus prepared the way for Mannix's rallying of the Irish in Australia.

Another example of someone who did not go along with the current was the (Anglican) Bishop Stephen of Tasmania during World War II. He suggested that Britain had taken territory forcibly in her past and hence both Germany and Britain needed to ask for divine forgiveness. But society and the press were not prepared to hear this talk since it threatened the received myth about the enemy.

One of the numerous anti-Mannix
cartoons of this period.

Archbishop Daniel Mannix depicted by car-
toonist L.F.Reynolds wearing his distinctive
top silk had and frock coat. Melbourne
Punch 12 March 1925.

A vital question: Will the Favourite Fall, and let the
imported outsider win?

Mannix as a cultural icon

Sir William Cullen warned that clergymen should not preach sermons 'directed towards modifying any spirit of resentment'.[140]

State aid for church schools was another issue espoused by Mannix which illustrates the way the individual can change the group. Early on in his time in Melbourne he stated that the lack of state aid in education was 'the one great stain upon the statute books of this free and progressive land'.[141] He was a bit of a rebel and his actions are an echo of the rebellious spirit of the Vinegar Hill uprising. One big difference was that by Mannix's era colonial society was more complex. The successful resolution to the school funding issue (as far as Catholics were concerned) came only much later after he had departed the scene, but he initiated the debate and brought it to a new intensity in spite of the fairly general persistence of the culture which denied funding. In this action his strength as a symbol of the subculture was evident. He again galvanised the Irish tribalism that was his support, reinforcing the subculture.

Opposition to funding re-emerged as the DOGS (Defence of Government Schools) movement in the late 1970s, culminating in an unsuccessful High Court challenge. This is a good example of the change in culture over time from one of general persistence of the culture of denying funding (perceived as an aspect of sectarianism, although free, secular and compulsory education was originally meant to be anti-sectarian!) to a modified sectional persistence which was overcome finally but not completely extinguished (DOGS).

However it must be said that as a churchman in Australian society, Mannix exercised on the culture an influence which few Australian bishops have ever matched. That could well be because he was not in the mould of the other Australian bishops in the nineteenth century and indeed in this century. John Molony makes the point in his book, *The Roman Mould of the Australian Catholic Church*[142] that the Catholic Church in Australia was formed in the Roman, not Irish mould from the time the hierarchy was set up in 1842. The Roman culture appointed bishops only in this religious mould (in a similar way Pope John Paul II appoints bishops who conform to a certain mould, often to the dismay of local hierarchies). Virtually all the bishops had been Roman-trained and were identified by their strong papal loyalty. Hence they were silently obedient whereas Mannix was outspoken and showed a strain of Irish Gallicanism (a certain independence of Rome) that was evident to all. There were two exceptions to the Catholic Irish bishops syndrome. Giovanni Cani became the first bishop of Rockhampton in 1882, and Elzear Torreggiani, with no local experience, became bishop of Armidale in 1879.

Breaking the Irish/ Roman mould: Giovanni (John) Cani, an Italian bishop.

The Roman mould would become very evident in the history of Australian Catholicism, concludes Molony, in the stand taken by the Catholic Church (bishops taking their cue from Pius IX) on temporal power, liberalism, freemasonry, education and relations with other churches.[143] (There is a mould for popes as well which occasionally is disregarded, as in the notable cases of Alexander VI and John XXIII, with historical consequences!)

Mannix's contribution to the dynamism of change and the persistence of the Irish/Catholic subculture was both dramatic and substantial.

From sectarianism to ecumenism

Another fascinating area of change is that of ecumenism. One of the things Mannix did not change, in fact exacerbated, was the sectarianism of his times. Edmund Campion has given us a vivid description of the sectarianism of earlier this century as has Frank Engels in his two volumes.[144]

The atmosphere of sectarianism which in most colonial countries perpetuated the divisions and feelings dating back to the Reformation and the Counter-Reformation, was there right from the beginning.

On the bright side, there were some impressive examples of ecumenism during World War I. James Green, a Methodist minister, shared quarters with a Capuchin friar for some time and he recalled how they spent much time in discussing their various theological positions. The same James Green and Anglican priest, A.E. Talbot, conducted a combined communion service at Gallipoli. A. Stevenson, a Presbyterian, wrote of a close friend and Catholic chaplain killed in the war: 'I shall never believe that a church which can produce such men is altogether evil'.[145] The war experience taught Australians that religion need not be a series of bitter and acrimonious fights.

Another noticeable exception to this sectarianism was the Prime Minister, Robert Menzies, who is, perhaps, another example of the individual bringing about change in the larger group. As the clouds of World War II gathered over Europe, Menzies, in a speech on 28 May 1939, to a crowd of sixty thousand assembled in Melbourne's Exhibition Building to demonstrate for peace, sounded an unusual ecumenical note, not unlike John XXIII would do twenty years later. He said:

> The things which bind us are greater than the things which divide. That is why I, a Presbyterian, can stand here, a non-Catholic, on a Catholic platform, because we all believe that our common Christian faith is greater than any differences of doctrine. All of us, non-Catholic and Catholic, believe that the essence of our Christian faith is in the fatherhood of God, and there can be no belief in the fatherhood of God without a real belief in the brotherhood of man.
>
> The task of statesmanship today is to get people to believe more in the things uniting them than in things keeping them apart...
>
> Let us begin now, and instead of talking of the inevitability of war, talk of the inevitability of peace...[146]

But after the wars the old negative attitudes continued down the years and in spite of the World Council of Churches (1948; hereafter WCC) and Vatican II (1962-5), many older Protestant and Catholics still see it this way.

Mannix was certainly not an ecumenist. On the contrary I think he might well have used sectarianism as a tool, albeit unconsciously, for promoting his other agenda - the persistence of the Irish/Catholic subculture. Not surprisingly in an address in 1914 on church unity Mannix said:

> Strife among Christians is painful and distressing; but worse still, peace bought by the barter of principles or of conscientious conviction. The man who would say that for peace he is prepared to compromise, to give way on this or that article of his creed, shows that in reality he has no convictions, no principle to give away.[147]

Later in 1929, he spoke out against any attempt to hold a combined church service with other denominations - the kind of attitude that led to prayer being banned on Anzac Day.

Thus Mannix reinforced those elements of the Irish/Catholic subculture that helped to keep it distinct from the (British) dominant culture. On the theoretical level, one can say that if this is not done then there is always the possibility that the subculture simply will melt into the dominant culture as it progressively loses those customs or cultural items that originally made it different from the dominant culture. In anthropological terms, Mannix very definitely helped the persistence of the culture.

Santamaria also gives examples of further ecumenical cooperation at a time when it was not common. He cites the case of the Movement (the combined action against communism led by Santamaria) working with other Christian people, like the Anglican, L. Biggs, and the Rev Palmer Phillips in hammering out a common policy with regard to socio-economic structures to be implemented after the war.[148]

These few examples of ecumenical spirit cited above are good examples of origination, that is, change coming from within the culture. Of themselves they were not enough to change the persistence of the sectarian culture yet they probably laid the groundwork for what was to come. The added weight of acculturation, which by definition is a change from without, was necessary. That came from the foundation of the WCC and Vatican II.

Diffusion among the churches in an ecumenical age

An interesting phenomenon associated with ecumenism is that of religious diffusion. With practice of inter-church dialogue and activities this century and especially since the foundation of the WCC and Vatican II, there have been many examples of the diffusion of elements of religious culture.

The use of bible study groups among Catholics would be one example of a custom that in some cases at least, they have learnt from the Protestants. Spontaneous praying (without set formulas) would be another, although the charismatic movement also helped to diffuse that practice. The decentralisation of parish responsibilities, as seen in the UCA with their system of elders, is something the Catholics are beginning to imitate, although that, too, has received encouragement from a theology of ministries that promotes collaborative approaches.

On the other hand some UCA ministers are beginning to use more symbols in their services and prayer sessions - something for which the Catholics, and more particularly the Orthodox, were known. Candles, icons, songs and sacred objects are being used more and more as aids to prayer. Even methods of meditation taken from Catholic and Orthodox traditions are being diffused. Among Catholics there is some use of the Orthodox icons, particularly the Byzantine images of Jesus. The Taizé music from France has been diffused among many denominations throughout the world.

The Irish-Catholic/Labor nexus broken

Pursuing our topic of change in its many forms, the link between Irish/Catholicism and the ALP is another example worthy of scrutiny because it highlights the interconnectedness of elements in a culture or subculture. In Victoria in the middle of the nineteenth century, religious affiliation seemed to be no problem in politics. The Catholics, John O'Shanassy and Charles Gavan Duffy, both became premiers. In spite of the close link between the Labor Party and Irish Catholics, the party was not able to support the issue of funding for Catholic schools because of opposition from Protestant leaders and from sections of the Labor Party itself.[149]

In Mannix's time, at the beginning of the twentieth century, the Labor Party became virtually synonymous with Irish Catholicism. That was not the case in the beginning. When the Labor Party was founded in 1891 there was equal support from Protestants (including evangelicals and Methodists[150]) and Catholics. Cardinal Moran encouraged the formation of the Labor Party (and of Federation). However the Protestant churches tended to get the label of wowsers for their support of the anti-drink and gambling campaigns and so tended to alienate the workers. The fact that many Protestants came from the wealthy echelons of society did not help.

This was unfortunate, given their support for many social reform ideas towards the end of the nineteenth century.

The conscription debate did not help the Protestant/Labor relationship either. The 'No-vote' was held by a numerically significant sector, represented particularly by the Labor movement and the Catholic Church. After the conscription showdown, when Hughes walked out of the Labor Party, the majority of those Laborites who stayed (whether parliamentarians or voters), were Catholics. The party was thus seen for many years afterwards as Irish and Catholic. 'Catholics, most of whom were working class, became the party's backbone, because they saw its concern for the poor and oppressed as an indicator of hope in their own depressed economic and social conditions.'[151] Labor presented itself as the party of the workers and underprivileged. Then all this subculture changed. But what caused it to change?

Undoubtedly the split in the 1950s was the main factor. When the Victorian industrial groupers realised that they did not have to remain in the ALP, they formed the Democratic Labor Party (DLP) and broke the umbilical cord which up to this point had bound Irish Catholics to the ALP.[152] (Hally comments that Catholic support for Labor probably would have begun to waver by the 1950s anyway as they moved up the social ladder.[153]) In anthropological terms, the trauma was the breaking of the socialisation mould of the Irish-Catholic/Labor family. The ghetto and tribal unity were shattered. Or in semiotic language, the cluster of symbols that once held a special web of meanings - Irish, Catholic, Labor, oppression, worker - lost its coherence.

Not only were the laity divided, but the Catholic bishops too. Whereas formerly loyalties were univalently to Irish-Catholicism and Labor, now other loyalties emerged such as those to one's local bishop, to Melbourne or Sydney, to political ideals or bishops, and to the national Catholic Church or the Vatican.

Aptly, the break has been described as the political coming of age of Catholics. It presented Catholics with an ideational challenge in so far as they had to re-think the meaning of Catholic Action and political action. In this sense the break helped bring the Irish-Catholics in to line with the rest of the Australian community - it assisted national unity.

Certain consequences followed the split. The split did away with political/religious stereotypes. Menzies' party had had only a handful of Catholics. Now Catholics could make choices across the spectrum of the parties.

Republicanism is another illustration of this concern. Mannix was accused of being disloyal to Britain and of encouraging other Catholics to do the same. However, other Catholic bishops were monarchists. Nevertheless some rather tenuously saw the line as being drawn between the Protestant monarchists and the Catholic republicans. Now this kind of alignment (if ever valid) is gone forever.

To express it in different terms: one ingredient of the Catholic or Protestant subculture was the political alignment. With political, economic and religious developments in the late nineteenth and twentieth centuries that ingredient is no longer considered essential to preserve the subcultures. Identities now rely on other factors. Catholics rely on their schools, their religious beliefs and practices, their adherence to the pope, and not insignificantly now, to their Australian icon Mary MacKillop. Different Protestant denominations have their own cultural elements. Among them the UCA is interesting in that recently (1977) it went through a re-organising of its religious symbols and probably is still in the process of stabilising those symbols.

All religious subcultures preserve their identity through testing and asserting their understanding of orthodoxy. I am not suggesting that it is done consciously to re-enforce identity but it does play that role. Some examples come to mind. I am thinking of the Presbyterian Church and the various enquiries as to the teachings of Samuel Angus (and in 1994 of Peter Cameron) that spanned a decade. In the Catholic Church (Frs) David Coffey (questioned about his writings on the resurrection) and Bill O'Shea (questioned about his explanations of Catholic doctrines) are two examples. A religious subculture always can use the charge of heresy to keep the ideational boundaries of the subculture clear and its teachings cohesive.

Change in the religious culture: decline of church attendance

One way to look at decline in a religious culture is to take the changing physical symbols of religion, the church buildings themselves. Where once the three major church buildings used to dominate the village square in the nineteenth century, now at least in the big cities, they have lost their physical and possibly their moral and spiritual prominence as well. This point is well made in the ABC documentary film, *Where the River Flows*, about how the churches in Australia are responding to change. St Francis of Assisi's in Melbourne CBD is one example. St George's or St Stephen's Presbyterian Church in Sydney are other examples. They are near Hyde Park and dwarfed by the surrounding buildings, as is St James's by the New Supreme Court skyscraper. The Great Synagogue in Elizabeth Street is no longer physically great. There would be many other examples if one looked.

The comparative decline of the physical profile of the church buildings is matched by the decline in church attendance. Both the fact of this decline and other demographic data are presented in Peter Kaldor's excellent book with the awkward title, *Who Goes Where? Who Doesn't Care?* [154]

His research is based on:

- Church and Census Data (1983-1986),
- the Australian Values Survey (AVSS, 1983),
- The McNair-Anderson Survey,
- some older survey data such as:
  - Roy Morgan surveys of 1960,1961, and 1966;
  - Australian Political Attitudes Survey, 1967,1979;
  - Age Poll, 1973;
  - Australian Gallup Polls, McNair-Anderson, 1976, 1980;
  - Mol 1966, published in 1971.

Some of his more important conclusions regarding patterns of church attendance up to 1984, which signal changing religious culture, can be summarised as follows:

* The period between 1960 and 1984 has seen not only a declining percentage of Australians claiming regular church attendance but also the changing face of those who do attend (p.24);

* The percentage of nominal Catholics has increased, largely due to the patterns of postwar migration. Mainline Protestants have declined in their share of the Australian population. At the same time the percentage not claiming any religious affiliation over the last ten to fifteen years has increased to nearly one quarter of the population (p.24);

* Non-attendance at church is not always related to unbelief or lack of religious orientation. There can be many reasons why people might choose not to be involved regularly in the public and institutional dimension of religious life, which reasons have little to do with religious orientation (p.38);

* In urban areas certain types of communities are likely to sustain large churches whilst in others, churches of all denominations are likely to be struggling. Mainline Protestant churches all tend to be stronger in stable dormitory suburbs which are of higher socio-economic status and have few people born overseas. Attendance rates are much lower in more diverse, multicultural or blue-collar communities. Catholic mass attendance rates are spread more widely although nominal Catholics are less likely to be regular attenders in areas of lower socio-economic status or where there are high percentages of people twenty to twenty-nine years of age.

* Attendance is higher in the smaller, stable rural communities and lower in more diverse, mobile or larger regional towns. Parishes with many twenty to thirty - year-olds in the community tend to have lower attendance rates. After adjustment for other factors it would

appear that there is a positive relationship between attendance rates and the socio-economic status of an area (p.93);

Factors affecting church attendance:

* All other factors being equal, increasing education is likely to increase participation in the churches. At the same time it is likely to erode orthodox Christian beliefs and perceptions of the relevance of the ten commandments. Those with little education are less likely to participate in church life but more likely to hold to orthodox Christian beliefs (p.127);

* People between twenty and forty years of age are poorer church attenders than any other age group. Further, they claim lower levels of orthodox Christian beliefs and religious experiences (p.146);

* People who have suffered any marital instability are less likely to attend church or have a religious orientation (p.146);

* People with children of school age appear more likely to attend church (p.146);

* Changing residence is likely to lower church attendance rates (p.172);

Kaldor's work is important in bringing to light the changes that have occurred in church attendance patterns and the many contributing factors. This is a valuable demographic and sociological contribution. The first point of significance is that these are facts, not hypotheses. There is still a partial persistence of the religious culture which denies that anything has changed thus allowing them to continue with old ways even though they are no longer effective.

A second point from Kaldor's research flows from the first. It is evident that the cultural composition of many parishes has changed and therefore their religious cultural identity as well. Churches, pastors and parish councils now have to work out the implications of all this for their diocese or parish. Acknowledgment of the fact, together with insights such as those provided by McKay and Lewins below regarding the interplay of groups, the process of change and the persistence of older customs, may be of help in pastoral planning.

The Catholic trauma of Vatican II

As a source for the study of religious change, Vatican II (1962-65) must rank high in the contemporary world. For many Catholics this council has proved most traumatic. Some say that the period of change from Vatican II till now has been unprecedented in the history of the Christian church as regards its rapidity and profundity. In reality it marked the Catholic Church's attempt finally to come to terms with the Enlightenment and modernity.

Coming from the early part of the century the scene was one of stability in theology and practices that could be said to go back (at least) to Pius IX and the doctrine of papal infallibility. From then on to the end of Pius XII's papacy in 1957, some would say authoritarianism prevailed with a great emphasis on papal loyalty. Church criticism was equal to disloyalty. Many believers felt a great feeling of stability and security. In anthropological terms, Catholicism had come to terms with its religious ideational environment some time previous to this, perhaps since Vatican I, and was enjoying reasonable ideational stability. Or, as Azevedo puts it, the church with Vatican I, 'consecrated the cultural "ghetto" attitude in which it had lived in the last centuries'.[155] This ghetto in reality pointed to a deep theoretical rift between the Catholic Church and those societies springing from the growing process of modernisation.

Vatican II, surprisingly initiated by a 'safe' candidate, John XXIII, was a traumatic experience in the life of Catholicism. It was traumatic because too many changes came too quickly with little or no explanation. This applies to both clergy and laity. Parish priests were required to turn the altar around with the priest facing the congregation for the first time. The prayers were to be in the vernacular, that is, in English for most people in Australia; responses were called for; people had to stand and kneel, sing and recite; communion was given on the hand and often by layfolk - a practice many thought was disrespectful; the Latin Gregorian chant often was replaced with psalms, songs and pop music to the accompaniment of guitars and other novel instruments.

Private confession which was speaking into a screen to an unseen person, either disappeared or gave way to a friendly face-to-face chat with the priest. (Culturally, private confession, or the first rite of reconciliation, continues with reduced frequency - which is a good example of the partial persistence of a religious cultural practice.) Morality seemed to have come down to personal choice whereas formerly the priest symbolised moral certitude. The ABC television series, *Brides of Christ*, portrayed this Catholic moral dilemma of the 1960s very convincingly.

The religious culture seemed to change overnight. It caused an enormous upheaval as people saw their religious symbols changed or removed. Many priests and religious left their religious orders and church attendance declined in the years of redefinition after Vatican II. The change was comprehensive enough to be seen as a case of rapid religious acculturation.

A new theology was born. What was theologically taboo in the 1950s became the new standard version of the 1960s. The gap was closing between the Enlightenment and the medieval church. Those theologians who had been frowned upon in the first part of the century were rehabilitated and became the *periti* (experts) of the Council! Rahner, Chenu, de Lubac, Congar, Schillebeeckx, Courtney Murray and others contributed to the new theological orientation of openness to other Christians, to other world religions and to the world, that underpinned much of the Vatican II documents.

It was soon evident that there were many who thought Vatican II was wrong in its new orientation and attempted to slow things down or reject them altogether, as did Archbishop Lefevbre who started up his own seminary in Switzerland. In other words, there was general persistence of pre-Vatican II religious culture. Some grieved over the loss of Latin and sought to continue celebrating the Eucharist in Latin as is done in Australia and elsewhere. Some added to this the use of the Tridentine Mass which, initially banned, was allowed later by John Paul II. Both are clear cases of both sectional (by a section of the population) persistence and partial (customs performed less frequently) persistence of a religious cultural custom. The two categories often overlap.

Other examples of sectional persistence of religious practices would be novenas, scapulars, sacred heart statues, and religious habits, while examples of partial persistence would include home visitation by priests, the parish 'mission', the four-hymn liturgies, the use of votive candles and clerical reticence towards the media. With all these examples I am thinking of the Catholic Church in the English-speaking world and more precisely, in Australia. Examples from other countries might well be quite different depending on their religious culture. There are examples from the UCA which we will mention below.

There are examples of 'survivals' (in the anthropological sense that was described in chapter 2) also dating from this period. Some examples would be, the communion rails, monstrances, holy cards with indulgences, and perhaps and to some extent, the stations of the cross, the ringing of bells before the elevation of the host during the Eucharistic celebration and crossing the forehead, lips and heart before the gospel is read.

Opposition to Vatican II continues especially among those who see what they would call the certainties of the past being betrayed. Groups known as Concerned Parents, Australian Catholics Advocacy Centre, CUF (Catholics United for the Faith) and others carry on a more or less strident campaign against the new trends.

These objectors represent a part of the religious culture that cannot adapt to a changing culture. They are resisting religious acculturation and seem to deny the essentially dynamic nature of all culture, including religious culture. As such they are illustrations of the general and partial persistence of a surpassed religious culture.

144 • RELIGION IN AUSTRALIAN CULTURE

Since Vatican II there has been a curious double movement. There has been a movement of convergence between Christian denominations on the one hand, and concomitantly a movement of divergence among adherents within the same denomination.

One way of looking at it, is that, in cultural terms, the *ideational* need which previously was met with a well thought-out system (pre-Vatican II Catholicism, neo-Thomism) into which the individual was socialised, suddenly was shattered with all the new ideas. Latin was gone, the priest faced the people, people were encouraged to read the bible, the ten commandments seemed to be neglected, Sunday non-attendance at Mass was no longer a mortal sin; some priests, instead of giving absolute answers to moral dilemmas, told parishioners to make up their own minds. It seemed to many that black was now white, white black, and in between an enormous and expanding sea of grey. People's ideational world had been shattered with no substitute readily available. The *integrative* role of religion in many cases ceased to exist. Catholicism seemed to have fallen apart.

During this period there are many examples of change which, if interpreted from an anthropological viewpoint, might be helpful. Examples from clerical life spring to mind. There are many systems of symbols which operate within a broader meaning system in the Catholic Church. One is the clerical club. Some symbols of this club are: priests, clerical dress, the roman collar, chalice, breviary, etc. This group is seen often as above and apart from the rest in the church. The culture of the group is handed down in the seminaries, a period when they are educated largely in isolation from the rest of humankind for a period of six or seven years.

Azevedo refers to the gap between 'the repetitively trained church leadership and the constantly evolving scientific mind of the modern laity'[156]. This training consolidates the group identity as regards their status while 'the faithful' put them on a pedestal. (Hence the resistance to any attempt radically to change the training of priests. They are right, a change might well change the culture of the club, perhaps making them less coherent as a club.) Up till now there has been a general persistence of the clerical club culture.

This group has presented itself to others through the above symbols. Since Vatican II some of these symbols have been changed. The laity often respond negatively to changes in clerical dress. Even the use of clay chalices, instead of silver sometimes threatens the meaning of the symbols. The wave of clerical sexual abuse in many countries has not helped to keep the symbols together.

As regards the alleged sexual abuse cases the clerical club (through the bishops) had to try to defend its identity, to keep the cluster of symbols intact, so they declined to comment or denied the reality. Later officials had to acknowledge what had happened often unconsciously betraying their clerical-mindedness, by mentioning only the perpetrator (cleric) and overlooking the victim. They saw the damage done to the clerical club. The victims and their relatives were outraged. In 1996 the Catholic bishops finally openly admitted the wrongs that had been done and apologised to the public. In the wake of this the cluster of symbols that made up the clerical state inevitably will be revised as the religious culture of the ordained changes.

Secondly the laity was divided. The reaction of one lay group paralleled the clerics: initial refusal to acknowledge but followed by a reluctant acceptance of the facts. A second group, perhaps anti-clerical in orientation, was quick to demand the whole truth and justice. Overall and after some time, it would seem that for all the laity, the original pattern of meaning regarding priesthood has been changed irrevocably. The pedestal by and large has gone.

What it means to be a priest is being re-defined. The traditional symbols have lost their meaning. New ones will have to be developed. David Walker, in a perceptive article,[157] calls for priests to strive single-mindedly to be the 'holy ones' of the community - but it is something they will have to earn. If this occurs then 'holiness' will form part of a new cluster of symbols that will indicate 'ordained minister or leader'. I doubt that clerical dress will be one, but 'chalice' well might be, provided that one of the duties of the priest continues to be to preside over the Eucharist.

The pattern of meaning called the clerical club overlaps with another pattern, that is, the one that includes members of religious orders. The symbols in this group are priests, male religious, female religious, habits, veil, and rosary, etc. Within this system the hierarchical worth of persons is: priests, male religious, female religious. They are separated from the rest, the laity. A hierarchical system as sharp as this is not common to all denominations in Australia. The Methodists, for one, had admitted laymen to their Conferences as far back as 1875 and the Anglicans have their synods with lay representation.

The overlapping of patterns of meaning is further evidenced by the 1994 Synod of Women in the Church where the possibility of female religious sharing decision-making in the church was discussed. In the overlapping pattern of symbols female religious have one foot in the inner circle by reason of being religious, but the other is outside the (clerical) camp because they are women. Under the force of the feminist movement the boundaries of some patterns of meaning are being threatened. Hence the strong opposition to the ordination of women taken for the moment from a purely anthropological viewpoint. The movement threatens the established ideational synthesis of the group (clerical club).

I see a change in the clerical club culture occurring currently from an interesting quarter. Through the diffusion of the practice of pastoral associates (people, often female religious, who work pastorally with the priest) the practice of collaboration in ministry is beginning to change the pre-Vatican II one. Meetings of priests and pastoral associates, regional or national, are both the sign and the fruits of this. On the other hand, the persistence of the old model is evidenced by those priests who continue to stay away from such meetings.

This latter change in the clerical club in the Catholic Church took place in the Presbyterian, Methodist and Congregational Churches in the 1950s to 1970s with the debates over women's ordination. Catholics could do well to learn from their experience that changes in religious culture, always painful, can be evolutionary and growth-promoting rather than catastrophic and terminal. One recalls the dictum about culture in general from an earlier chapter: culture, and therefore religious culture, is by definition dynamic and changing.

The spirituality prior to Vatican II had its own symbols. There were the rosary, benediction, novenas, etc. These have been modified, leaving some people in distress. Here and there old symbols persist as survivals in the anthropological sense. But the world of meaning through these symbols has disappeared largely.

Another example is communion. The old symbols were: priest, communion rails, kneeling, tongue. All these suggested holiness and respect. The new symbols including layfolk, standing, and host in the hand, is seen by some to mean a lack of respect and a devaluation of the ritual.

For those who can find a new synthesis, religion can play a new integrative role; for those who cannot manage to change, there is confusion, despair, or a renewed commitment to a strident conservatism which is another way of holding on to one's old ideational synthesis, or persisting with the old religious culture. This latter becomes increasingly more difficult to do as the religious acculturation becomes more general.

The Uniting Church in Australia and change

The UCA which was formed in 1977 from the Congregational, Methodist and Presbyterian Churches, knows about change in a very experiential and often painful way. The Methodist tradition is English and working class in its origins, whereas the Presbyterian and Congregational Churches are more middle class in their origins and certainly the Presbyterian Church traces its genesis to Switzerland and Calvin in the sixteenth century. After 1977 some Presbyterian parishes continued as Presbyterian Churches, whereas all the Methodist and all the Congregational parishes voted to form the UCA.

What I would like to do now is to illustrate different kinds of change that one can find in the UCA. Hopefully this will help all concerned in understanding the process of religious change in the place where they work and worship.

One example of sectional persistence in the UCA is the time of celebrating the Eucharist. In the Presbyterian Church, communion, or the Lord's Supper, was celebrated quarterly. This was done at 8.30am in one particular church. Since 1977 this UCA minister (formerly Presbyterian), has been celebrating the Lord's Supper monthly and at different timeslots on a Sunday. Every quarter however it is done at 8.30am in his particular parish!

Another example of sectional persistence is the word used for the house where the minister resides. The name used tends to be the name used by the original church in that place. So if the church was formerly a Presbyterian or Congregational Church it is called a 'manse', if Methodist a 'parsonage'.

When it comes to the actual way or style in which the Lord's Supper is celebrated it tends to be done in the style of the tradition from which the minister comes. I am told that the older parishioners can pick out whether the style is 'Presbyterian' or 'Methodist'. The Congregational style is too close to Presbyterian to distinguish differences.

The Presbyterians have a tradition of the benediction, that is, of asking someone present, usually the minister to give the verbal benediction (blessing) at the end of a prayer session, bible study or meeting. This custom often persists where former Presbyterians are in the group. The session is felt to be incomplete without the benediction.

The Presbyterian/Congregational custom was to show respect in a church by silence and strict decorum while the Methodist usage was one of more informality tolerating talking and greeting others especially during the 'passing of the peace' (known as 'the sign of peace' in Catholic liturgy). In the UCA now the latter approach is the more prevalent. Where the quieter approach exists one would have an example of sectional persistence of an element of the religious culture. (This particular example has its parallel in the Catholic Church based along ethnic lines: the Anglo-Celtic and Northern European cultures tend to be silent in church while the southern Europeans regard God's house as theirs too.)

There are also examples of partial persistence, that is, where a religious custom is performed less frequently. The custom or tradition of preaching is one example. The style of preaching differed among the churches. The Presbyterian Church has a proud record of very well-prepared academic sermons while the Methodists were more along the lines of the social gospel, or at its worst, moralising. Since union, according to some, the Presbyterian style has all but vanished; where it is to be found still it would be an example of partial persistence.

Examples of partial persistence are not all that easy to find. One which will die out fairly soon is associated with the sick and elderly. One UCA (former Presbyterian) minister uses the *Book of Common Order* of the Presbyterian Church when he attends the sick and elderly of the UCA who were formerly Presbyterians. The prayers they knew as children and young adults and the particular language used are all forms of the old and familiar which give comfort and consolation to these people as they near their journey's end. As the younger generation grows up they will never use these prayers because they will never have known them.

Western cultural changes in the 1960s

The 1960s also represented changes in culture generally best epitomised in the student uprisings around the world and in Paris, in particular, in May-June 1968. It is difficult to summarise what was at the core of this shift but some ideas can be named. It included the sexual revolution that was sweeping the world, at least the developed world and the beginnings of feminism with writers like Germaine Greer, Simone de Beauvoir, and Mary Daly. Values like the dignity of the individual, greater personal freedom especially sexual freedom, greater autonomy for the person, rejection of blind obedience, and rational argumentation rather than dogmatism were nurtured.

This revolution had its effects on religion and the impact of those still are seeping into the ecclesiastical structures. One vivid example of the changes taken from Catholicism was the reaction to the encyclical, *Humanae Vitae*, which, in spite of many powerful insights into conjugal love, is known better by some as the document that ruled out contraception. In the 1870s and later, Catholics would have obeyed without murmur. In 1968, when the document was released by Paul VI, they heard what was said but made their own decisions and often publicly disagreed with the pope's teaching. This was symptomatic a big turning point in the moral authority of the pope.

Hugh Mackay is one commentator who traces these general trends of the 1960s in Australia and now sees the people of the 1990s as going back to basics in some ways.

The influence of religion on culture?

Other than Mannix, what representatives of denominations or religions have exercised any influence on the general culture of the society? Some I believe, although it is not easy to measure the interaction of religion and culture. Hally is of the opinion that as so many of the population in Australia are Christian it is unthinkable that they would not have had some influence on the general culture as well as vice versa.[158] One example quoted is the way the churches promoted democracy and justice in Australia. A document was produced in 1994 by the Commonwealth government entitled *Whereas the People - Civics and Citizenship Education Report* which proposed to educate students in the history of democracy and justice in Australia. The problem is that no mention is made of the churches' contribution and some denominations have reacted sharply to this inadequate perspective. A list of names will show quickly that this is a serious omission. All these people and others have contributed in various ways to democracy, social justice, nationalism and education: Richard Johnson, Bede Polding, John Dunmore Lang, Caroline Chisholm, John Plunkett, Mary Lee (Women's Christian Temperance Union), Congregations of the Catholic sisters and brothers, William Duncan, John West, Patrick Moran, Alfred Deakin, Alan Walker, R.B.S. Hammond, E. H. Burgmann and Frank Brennan[159].

The influence of religion on governments, public bodies, personal life, community attitudes, popular culture, and national priorities often is very subtle. The way members of Parliament might be influenced by their (or others') religious convictions is difficult to determine. Nevertheless as we look at history some instances can be cited.

On 11 November 1951, fifty years after Federation, there was the historical 'Call to the People of Australia' pointing out the dangers facing the country. Among those who signed the document were six prominent judges and the leaders of the Anglican, Catholic, Presbyterian and Methodist Churches as well as the Australian Council of Churches. It was a call to restore the moral order in the context of a strong anti-communist crusade and the occurrence of the Korean War. As Hogan points out, it shows the traditional close relationship between magistrates and church leaders who saw their roles as the moral guardians of society.[160] Using the language of social conservatism, it maintains that the social order depends on a traditional moral order.

This strand of conservatism has reappeared in the 1980s' political party in NSW, known as the 'Call to Australia'. It sees its role as defending traditional moral values as defined by the Festival of Light and has the Rev Fred Nile as one of its leaders. What is of interest to note here is that the traditional rivalry between Catholics and Protestants has been set aside to confront the common foe of moral disorder in the guise of issues such as abortion, euthanasia, homosexuality, casinos, etc.

Although Breward says that few of Australia's church leaders made any significant contribution to the economic debates of the 1920s,[161] one can quote a few examples of recent times where church leaders have spoken out. In 1963 pressure was brought to bear on the Commonwealth to provide funds for science laboratories and libraries for church schools. In 1969 the Commonwealth began per capita grants to Catholic and independent schools. For some this would be an example of the way religion (Catholicism in this case) finally brought pressure to bear on the political system. Polding and Mannix in particular, and others would have rejoiced that their efforts finally had been brought to fruition.

In 1970/71 the Anglican Archbishop of Sydney, Sir Marcus Loane, drew the government's attention to the extent and depth of poverty in Australia.[162] William McMahon, Prime Minister at the time, challenged him to produce the evidence which he subsequently did. This, in turn, led to the Henderson Inquiry into poverty which established useful poverty indicators.

Coming up to the 1993 federal elections some churches objected to the GST (Goods and Services Tax) of the Liberal Party on the grounds that the poor would end being penalised more than others. This hurt the liberals. The UCA's social responsibility commission is constantly critiquing government policy. The Catholic Bishops' statement *Common Wealth and Common Good* has had some influence but difficult to quantify.

In 1994, *The Catholic Weekly*[163] published a letter signed by Edward Cardinal Clancy of the Catholic Church, Archbishop Keith Rayner, Primate of the Anglican Church of Australia, Commissioner John Gowans, Territorial Commander of the Salvation Army, Rev D'Arcy Wood, President of the Assembly of the UCA, Isi Leibler, President of the Executive Council of Australian Jewry, Dr Omar Lum, President of the Federation of Islamic Councils, and Robert Fitzgerald, President of the Australian Council of Social Services. The letter was addressed to the Prime Minister, Paul Keating, expressing the opinion that the government should give special attention to the plight of the unemployed, especially the long-term unemployed. It calls on the government to implement a five-year plan 'of substantial and sustained action' to reduce unemployment.

It is impossible to measure the impact of ecumenical and interfaith action such as this. What we do know is that politicians still fear the opposition of churches and faiths, and sooner would have them on side. That is at least some evidence that religion is an important and vital factor in the amalgam that makes up Australian culture. One has only to reflect on the ecumenical response to the Port Arthur massacre in April 1996 to realise the strength of religion in Australian culture.

The churches continue to play the role of reminding governments about values, especially that economic rationalism has its blind spots. In February 1994, the NSW Ecumenical Council hosted the Chilean 'barefoot economist' Professor Manfred Max-Neef. In a breakfast address to community leaders in Sydney he pointed out that Australia still could check the trend to economic rationalism that was ruining many other countries as was seen by dying European villages and increased city slums. Small local industries for the local market should be kept going while high technology industries could service the export industries.

Has religion influenced the law in Australia? According to some it has influenced common law through its adherence and promotion of the ten commandments and Christian virtues in general as a basis of common life. Jennifer Corkhill says:

> The profound influence of the Christian Church on the development of Australian law must be recognised. Almost two-thirds of the Australian population identi-

fy as Christian and, whether or not they conform to the prevailing system of beliefs and practices, they are bound to be influenced by its images and ethical codes.[164]

She makes the point in connection with article 37 of the Australian Sex Discrimination Act which grants protection to religious bodies. It provides a permanent statutory exemption for religious bodies regarding the ordination and training of ministers and priests. That this was granted is evidence that the churches have enormous influence over the formulation of law in Australia, says Corkhill.

Here it is not so much that a subculture, Christianity, is influencing the dominant culture but that Christianity, either implicitly or explicitly, is part of the dominant culture.

Another example in Australia is that of Muslims who want to get the divorce laws changed to accommodate better their religion. The present laws, they say, were drawn up with Christianity in mind. Success in this would indicate some influence of religion on the law.

Attitudes portrayed by the church are bound to flow over into society and to affect the perceptions and experiences of both adults and children. The liquor laws were a case in point. Religion was involved in both sides of the argument, whether to leave the hotels open till ten pm or keep the closing time at six pm. The laws on homosexuality were influenced by the churches' attitude and teaching about homosexuality.

On the other hand, the abolition of capital punishment was not church-inspired (some churches spoke in its favour) and the liberalisation of the divorce laws under Lionel Murphy went ahead in spite of the protestations of the churches. We also know that the UCA leaders were not able to make their influence felt in Queensland when they opposed mining at Aurukun in 1978.[165] The Premier, Sir Joh Bjelke-Petersen who was a committed Lutheran, referred to the opposition in the customary language of those times, as 'communists' stirring up the people. For the Lutheran-based religion of Bjelke-Petersen, religion and politics were to be kept separate.

Of course the influence does not always move in the direction: religion➤culture. When local culture influences religion there is always the possibility of inculturation but while the enthnocentric attitude generally prevailed among Christian missionaries in Australia, little or no inculturation occurred. Now we have signs of it in Australian hymns and liturgies (such as the use of the smoking ceremony in the Catholic Eucharist; and art in churches and in ceremonies as promoted by the Nungalinya College of the Uniting Church in the Northern Territory) and in the emerging Australian theology of writers like Banks, Wilson, Edwards, Fletcher, Stockton, Kelly, Brown, and Thornhill. It has been a long time in coming because of the prevalence and persistence of ethnocentrism in the West and a lack of input from the cultures and their representatives.

One notes the impact of the move to take more seriously indigenous culture which has missiological reasons as well as the decline of ethnocentrism.

**Inculturation was slow in coming:
Fr Phillip Zadro blessing the Fleet**

The ethnic factor

While considering changes in religious culture (Anglo-Celtic) a further complication is added by the addition of the ethnic factor. Here one now has a changing dominant culture (Anglo-Celtic), the interaction of the dominant culture with subcultures as well as the fact that these subcultures are themselves changing. Some of the complexity is illustrated by McKay and Lewins[166] who have made an interesting study of the various ways these factors have interrelated. They make use of the sociological interpretive model of Schermerhorn. It is worth describing it in full so as to appreciate how the Australian data can be related thereto (cf Figure 3).

Figure 3

Reciprocal goal definitions of centripetal and centrifugal trends of subordinates, as viewed by themselves and superordinates.

Cp = ideology preferring centripetral goals for subordinates
Cf = ideology preferring centrifugal goals for subordinates.

	A	B	
As viewed by superordinates	Cp	Cf	Facilitating integration
As viewed by subordinates	Cp	Cf	
	Assimilation incorporation	or Cultural pluralism or sanctioned autonomy	

	C	D	
As viewed by superordinates	Cf	Cp	Facilitating conflict
As viewed by subordinates	Cp	Cf	
	Forced segregation with resistance	Forced assimilation with resistance	

(source: Black, 167.)

Centripetal goals are those that overtly or covertly force subordinates to assimilate into dominant institutions. *Centrifugal* goals are those that sustain degrees of social and/or cultural compartmentalisation between themselves and subordinates. Where the goals of the dominant group and those of the subordinate group correspond there is integration and where the goals differ one has conflict.

Applying this to the Lebanese Catholics and Orthodox, McKay and Lewins conclude that they fit in to cell A of the above theoretical framework. Lebanese acquiescence to forces of anglicisation (married Anglo-Australians) and Latinisation ('Catholic' rather than 'Maronite', 'Melkite'or 'Orthodox') has resulted in second and third generation descendants having only residual and ephemeral feelings of Lebanese identity.

The Ukrainian Catholics fit into cell D originally. The Australian Catholics had centripetal goals (openness) while the Ukrainians had centrifugal goals (closed institutions) which led to conflict. More recently the Australian Catholics have modified their goals to be more centrifugal and thus Cell B is a better model for the current situation. For example, in 1958 the Ukrainian Catholics gained independence from the Latin-rite bishops with the establishment of the Ukrainian Exarchate in Australia. [167]

Polish and Croatian Catholics go into cell D where the Australian Catholics goals have been centripetal and assimilative, whereas the Poles and Croats desire to maintain their specific national religious practices, i.e., are centrifugal in their goals.

The Italians fit into cell C where the superordinates have centrifugal goals and the subordinates centripetal ones. The Italians wish to participate in parish life as *Italians* whereas the Australian Catholics wish to incorporate them as *Australian* Catholics and exclude them as *Italians*. The background to this is that Rome permitted ethnic groups to have their own chaplains, but the

Australian bishops resisted and positively promoted dispersion of ethnic groups into established parish communities so that they could be 'Australianised'.[168]

From this study it becomes quite clear how complex the interaction of religious and ethnic forces is in these cross-cultural situations and how invalid generalisations can be.

With the passing of sectarianism between Christian denominations, a new phenomenon has appeared. With the wave of migrants just after World War II, other world religions appeared in greater numbers. Buddhists from South East Asia, some Hindus from India, many Muslims from the Middle East and Bosnia settled in Australia and re-defined the religious scene. Some of the differences between Christian denominations now looked minor in the presence of more than a dozen mosques and temples where previously there had been only churches (with a synagogue or two). The new religions impinged very definitely when city councils were presented with development plans for a mosque, or workers sought a prayer room at the factory.

Summary

In this chapter the phenomena of diffusion and acculturation has been seen through many occurrences in the twentieth century in Australia. Mannix, for example, attempted to diffuse certain ideas through the community such as the idea that the Irish should improve their status, the 'No-vote' in the conscription debate, state aid for Catholic schools, and republicanism. His actions and words guaranteed the persistence of the Irish subculture.

Ecumenism diffused throughout the Protestant churches this century and throughout Catholicism especially since Vatican II. In fact it could be seen as religious acculturation so profound is it. It continues to change the face of institutionalised religion in Australia.

Other big changes in the religious scene were the break in the Irish-Catholic/Labor Party link, Vatican II and the formation of the UCA. There were many examples of general and partial persistence of pre-Vatican II religious culture. All this happened against the background of diffusion and acculturation in society in general in many countries from the 1960s: the questioning of authority and blind obedience, the sex revolution, feminism and an emphasis on self-fulfilment or 'doing one's own thing' - often a tendency to hedonism in short. An added complication to these debates in Australia is the multifaceted aspect of the culture and the interplay of different ethnic groups on each other on the one hand, and between them and the dominant culture on the other.

We also considered the possible influence of institutionalised religion on society, especially on topics like health care, taxation, family allowances, the Sex Discrimination Act and economic rationalism.

Points to ponder:

1. Can you give examples of religious diffusion and acculturation?

2. Give examples of general and partial pre-Vatican II or pre-Uniting Church religious customs.

3. Give examples of customs called 'survivals', that is, the persistence of practices that have lost their religious meaning.

4. To what extent, in your experience, can ecumenism be called an instance of religious acculturation?

5. Has the way older people have spoken about Vatican II or the formation of the UCA led you to see it as traumatic?

6. Do you think church leaders/clergy/believers should seek to influence public opinion? Why or why not? If yes, how should they do it?

6

Religious culture and the media

A word on methodology

Before I launch into this chapter, it might be useful to point out:

1. why the selected topic is 'the media'

2. how the methodology is somewhat different from that used in the preceding two chapters

1. I am focusing on a contemporary topic - the media - which is part of the wider concept of Australian culture. It is just one of many possible areas, or subsets to investigate, and I chose it because it is a striking manifestation of modernity, and because it plays a major role in the processes of enculturation, diffusion, acculturation and change.

2. The methodology is different.

• I take an element of the culture - the media - and another element of culture - religion - and investigate their mutual relationship within the general framework of culture as outlined at the end of chapter 3, and with specific mention of anthropological insights when appropriate.

• I attempt to describe what the media is and to identify its positive and negative values.
• I do an overview of some important church documents and writings from other experts in a largely bib-

liographical approach, while in chapters 4 and 5, historical events and people were the examples of cultural phenomena.

• I identify the actual relationship between religion and the media, by looking at the facts as we know them.

• I describe and evaluate the attempt religion has made to relate to media.

• I make a judgment as to the challenges for the religious media in the immediate future.

What is the media?

Throughout this chapter the emphasis will tend to be on television, rather than other forms of the media, because of its dominance in our culture. The media, as was pointed out in the *Introduction* to this book, is an important factor in the enculturation of all Australians. In addition to this the constant exposure to aspects of culture from abroad through the media means that people are vulnerable to both diffusion and acculturation. In particular, one would not be surprised if television played a major role in the acculturation of Aborigines to western values.

Let me begin with a simple anecdote. Many years ago our eldest child who was about six years old at the time, was watching television. On the news that particular evening there was an item on the birthday of the then Prime Minister, Malcolm Fraser. They showed shots of the celebrations with the cake and candles and everyone singing. 'Why's that on the news?', my daughter asked, 'that's happy'. The news on television had become synonymous with bad news in her mind.

This incident reminds us that the media can mean different things to different people. They may equate television with bad news or sex and violence and the radio with talkback shows, radio quizzes, or classical music. Usually by the plural word 'media' we mean all the electronic and print ways used to communicate publicly within and with society. The most common means are those of television, video, radio, newspapers, magazines, and advertising. Nichols goes further and includes closed circuit television, billboards, direct mail, E-mail, church bulletins and parish papers.[169] Others make the distinction between the *mass* media, intended for the public at large (television, radio, newspapers, etc.), and *alternative* media, intended for a limited audience (slides, cassettes, folk forms of communicating, etc).

In addition let me point out now the way Catholic Church documents often speak of 'the means of social communication' rather than 'the mass media'. The former way of speaking brings out the social dimension of the activity - we are, after all, speaking about *human beings* communicating, whereas 'mass media' places the emphasis on the things, the technology, and thereby dehumanises the activity.

The importance of a social dimension

Now let us ask ourselves what values the media promotes. In attempting to answer this question, I will be referring to official church documents as well as other writers such as Paul Duffy who in his helpful book, *Word of Life in Media and Gospel*[170] gives us a good overview of media values.

Positive values

Some of the values that the media promotes are positive values, others quite destructive. We can gather the evidence together by examining church documents and referring to other writings.

Among the positive values that Duffy mentions is the companionship that the radio ('the intimate companion') offers to elderly or house-bound people. It does this often by way of numerous talkback or music programs. On television there are comedy shows that promote family values or the soapies that show ordinary men and women working their way through common difficulties to greater maturity, as Duffy points out. There are also informative documentaries and educational programs.

As regards the official documents of the churches, what have they said about the positive value of the media, and in particular about television? Within Catholicism, prior to Vatican II and prior to the wide dissemination of television, Pius IX, impressed by the implications of modern technology, referring to 'the remarkable invention of Marconi' issued a radio message to 'all nations and every creature'.[171] Pius XII referred to the media as 'gifts of God',[172] and developed the idea of the good seed (good use of the media) and the evil seed (the evil use of the media) in his letter. Television can strengthen the 'bonds of loyalty and love within the family circle', provided the screen displays nothing 'which is contrary to those same virtues of loyalty and chaste love'.[173] However, it was really Vatican II that came out with a developed statement about the media.

The Vatican II *Decree on the Means of Social Communication* (known in Latin as *Inter mirifica*[174]), suggests that the laity in the media will 'animate' the media with a Christian and human spirit. One has only to watch the commercial stations in particular today to know how difficult this is. The document is clear on the church's task regarding the media which 'involves employing the means of social communication to announce the good news of salvation and to teach people how to use them properly.'(art 3) Just how this is to be done is another question.

Eight years later, *The Pastoral Instruction*[175] (in Latin, *Communio et Progressio*) has some positive things to say about the media:
• they are 'gifts of God' (art 1, repeating Pius XII's phrase);
• not to use the media would be 'burying the talents given by God'(art 123.);
• sees the media as bringing people closer together, promoting well being and unity, resolving fears, (art.6);
• their role is one of improving the human condition and contributing to human unity (art.9);
• encouraging social relations (art.12)
• contributing to 'the pursuit of truth' (art.13).

(The WCC Uppsala Report supported the use of the media as 'the agora and town meeting of technological

society'). The document makes the distinction between
- the communicators
- those who employ the media (the media barons)
- the recipients, commonly and significantly called 'consumers' in the secular context.

The doctrinal conviction that lies at the base of this
approach is that humankind was given the task of
'possessing and mastering the world' (Genesis 1:26-28;
9:2-3; Wisdom 9:2-3; and *Gaudium et Spes*, art 34). On the
other hand, the reality of original sin and our resultant
wounded humanity mean that we have constantly to
guard against the baser sides of our humanity exploiting
the media (if we are communicators) and being
exploited by the media (if we are recipients). With the
media, and especially television, there is always the
danger of encouraging 'mental idleness and passivity'
(art 21).

The danger of mental idleness and passivity

The *Pastoral Instruction* upholds the right of free speech for individuals and groups ('real freedom to speak their minds'), mentioned in article 26 and again in 116. It should be encouraged within the limits of the common good and public morality, says the document. The question of national identity, which is always relevant to Australia, is taken up in article 51 which stresses the role the media can play in impressing upon a nation its cultural identity. In anthropological terms it can play an important role in enculturation for those who grow up in Australia, and in diffusion and acculturation especially in the case of migrants and refugees. Advertising was identified as being on the increase in 1971 whereas today we might say that it has taken over in many cases. Fore talks about television being all about broadcasters 'delivering whole audiences to their sponsors'.

By 1971 the momentum for ecumenism in the Catholic world was gaining pace, having received its initial impetus from the enthusiasm of John XXIII and Vatican II. Not surprisingly therefore, the *Pastoral Instruction* points out that media action can have ecumenical or interfaith dimensions (art 99). Again in this document, the laity are seen to play the role of yeast in the bread, so to speak. Catholics within the system can help news editors not to overlook items of religious significance (art 103). Other than saying that the Church could find the media of great help in their efforts to announce the Word of God to modern men and women, no mention is made of televangelism, which by the time of the publication of the *Pastoral Instruction*, was already into its third generation of evangelists.

The Pontifical Council for Social Communication marked the twentieth anniversary of the *Pastoral*

Instruction with *Dawn of a New Era* (in Latin, *Aetatis Novae*) in 1992. This document is quite different in some respects. Initially it seems to be doing nothing more or less than going over old ground with a bow in the direction of modern technologies such as satellites, cable television, fiber optics, video cassettes, compact disks, computerised image-making and digital technology. However it seems someone pointed out that the problem partially lies in the episcopal conferences, patriarchal assemblies, dioceses, bishops and others not knowing what to do about the media, when all is said. This is supported by the repetition of familiar ideas since the *Decree on the Means of Social Communication*. Now, in this document, if only in the appendix, the 'how-to-do-it' package is spelt out with praiseworthy thoroughness.

The necessary elements include a vision statement, assessment of the local media environment, a proposed structure for church-related social communications, media education, outreach to media professionals, and last but not least, adequate financial support.

The elements are not enough, so the process of how to go about doing something concrete is broken down into a research phase (needs assessment, information gathering, analysis of strengths and weaknesses of the Church's current structures and programs), and then a design phase which addresses education, spiritual formation and pastoral care, cooperation with appropriate bodies, public relations, research, and finally, communications and development of peoples. This appendix provides a very clear map of both the content and the process - something earlier documents did not do, and probably could not through lack of expertise.

One should also mention two encyclicals which mention the media in passing. Paul VI's *Evangelii Nuntiandi* in 1976 repeats the call to use the media in preaching the gospel. Later in 1991, *Redemptoris Missio* of John Paul II asks for a greater understanding of the social role it plays and the need to integrate communication in the overall pastoral plan of the Church.

The WCC has also had something to say on the topic.[176] The reports from the General Assemblies of Uppsala (1968) and Vancouver (1983) devote special attention to the topic, whereas the other reports mention the media only in passing. The Uppsala report backgrounds the media in the daily lives of people and its impact on the Church. It also provides theological reflection on the interconnectedness of communication and all aspects of revelation, the Incarnation and Trinity. Questions about the domination of the media are raised and the need to train church people to understand the media better.

The Vancouver report of the WCC mentions both positive and negative aspects of the media and supports the demand of the South for a New World Information and Communication Order. It stresses that credibility should characterise church communication built on justice. It also, like so many church documents, calls for better training in the media and the integration of communication studies in the theological training programs.

The US Churches of Christ issued a document in 1992 through its National Council, entitled *Global Communication for Justice*. As the title indicates, there is plenty in this document on the Third World and the injustices inflicted on it through inadequate and incorrect reporting. Concentration of media ownership, coverage of developing countries, support for the voices of the oppressed, the right of all peoples to their own style of communication, advertising and entertainment, are some of the issues raised. Like Pius XII back in 1957, it mentions the media as God's gift and stresses its use in praising and glorifying God.

In addition to these documents, Bouma, a sociologist, is worth quoting. He sees the big picture. The media can provide meaning for life's questions. In his words:

> The media provide one source of answers to questions of meaning. Much of what is taken to be entertainment involves the rehearsal of answers to questions about the meaning of life. In an earlier age the church service and sermon was the single most commonly attended source of entertainment and information outside the home. Now television sitcoms show the triumph of good over evil, recount tales of greater or lesser heroism, show the value of unselfish giving, and the meaningfulness of life. Entertainment has become a major source of meaning. In fact the various television soaps are designed to reinforce different values. For example, *Neighbours* puts a greater stress on family than does *E Street*.[177]

On the evidence of these writings it is clear that the media has many positive values such as providing companionship, entertainment, information and promoting the unity of all humankind. Like many technological advances, the media is ambivalent in its value. Having looked at some of the positive values, we turn our attention now to the dark side, about which there seems to be plenty to say.

Negative values

Pius XI in *Vigilanti cura* in 1936[178] wrote to the Catholic hierarchy of the USA concerning films and warned against their dangers. He told the bishops to set up offices to promote morally decent films, to classify all films and make the classification known to all 'priests and faithful'. Pius XII celebrated the arrival of television with great joy but also wanted 'to protect the children from every danger' because of ' the great influence (of television) on the manner of thinking and acting of individuals and of every group of men'. This is interesting in that research is still trying to work out what exactly the relationship is.

The style of Pius XII is one that assumes that Christian morality is the only standard for society. It is the duty of the listener to select radio programs carefully, he points out.[179] Given the European setting in which he wrote, he was probably right at that time for Europe. The onus is on priests who have 'the care of souls' to have a sound knowledge of all questions which confront the souls of Christians regarding the media. The need for guidelines and censorship with a Catholic/Christian morality in mind (the functional role of religion) is the backdrop to this encyclical which assumes all along that ecclesiastical authority is going to be heeded. This indeed was still the case in the 1950s.

The Vatican II *Decree on the Means of Social Communication* is quick to mention the ambiguous nature of the media and stresses its danger. It sees its duty 'to treat of the main problems posed by the means of social communications (art 2). By this time (1963), television was available in most first-world countries at least and its potential for better or worse was becoming increasingly obvious to all. Not that the *Decree on the Means of Social Communication* failed to see the positive side, as was pointed out above.

What, one may wonder, has been the overall impact of these church documents? In general, Soukup is pessimistic about the value of church documents. He points out that the documents often simultaneously address the broad issue of the media in society and the narrower concerns of the Church's use of the media in a confusing way. Often too, the target audience of the documents is unclear; sometimes the shotgun approach seems to be used with multiple targets - all those of good will, civic leaders, Catholics, Catholics who work in the media, all Christians, governments, etc. His conclusion however is that few in the churches pay any attention to them anyway. He points out that the same ideas, good as they are, are often repeated with 'sad regularity'. However he thinks they are best used as starting points for further discussion, rather than taken as conclusions.[180]

Let us return to the negative side of television and see what others say. The first problem, according to O'Kelly, is that the world of television is not real. The culture and reality which it creates is often an unreal world as O'Kelly has shown by referring to a report, *Media Studies*, of the South Australian Department of Education.[181] Some examples of the unreal world of television according to this report are: in a typical week the viewer will see thirty police officers, seven lawyers, three judges, twelve nurses and ten doctors, but only one engineer or scientist. Service or manual workers comprise ten per cent of the screen population, but are sixty five per cent of the world. Men outnumber women three to one on the screen. The popular male age on television is from thirty to fifty five, but for women it is twenty to thirty. The television world is obsessed with crime; young males are seldom victims in violent scenes; the role of medicine is almost deified; and so it goes on, creating a world that does not match up to reality. As O'Kelly points out, one has to be critically aware of these distortions.

The world of television is unreal and the values that are promoted are often problematic, continues O'Kelly. Television shows can, for example, promote violence as the solution to all problems, they can depict a distorted idea of love as selfishness and sex. This serious dimension will be returned to shortly when contrasting gospel values and television values. The whole question of values, let it be said in passing, is central to any critical media education program be it for adults or children.[182]

Other than projecting an unreal world and undesirable values, television supplants religion. Horsfield[183] has written with great clarity and conviction on how television has, for a large proportion of the Australian population, taken over the role that religion plays in a person's life. He examines this proposition in terms of the three universal expressions/functions of religious faith: the practical (ritual, worship), the sociological (the system of social relationships) and the theoretical (beliefs). He takes 'religion' in the 'limit situation' meaning of David Tracy (those dimensions of life that go beyond the explanation, prediction or control of individuals).

As regards ritual and worship, he maintains that traditional religious worship transcends the present profane time. As opposed to this, television transcends time in the sense of entertainment and escape. Traditional worship is repetitive, with the same prayers being repeated (rosaries or psalms, hymns). Television has its own brand of repetitiveness. Soap operas repeat the same story over and over; jingles, sporting events and current affairs are noted for their sameness.

The second main function of religion is the sociological one. Traditionally religion provided meaningful social interaction for its adherents. Today television simply drugs its adherents into inaction. Where religion provided the tools of mystery, revelation and tradition to probe the supernatural, television provides fantasy and humour. The supernatural heroes called saints are now replaced with the news anchorpersons, who are cool and seemingly in control of everything: Mary Kostakidis, Brian Naylor, Heather Ford, Roger Young, David Johnston, Anne Sanders and others. Crime - , drama - or sports heroes are another form of the same; they are people who overcome all threats and restore order and harmony - like the saints.

Thirdly, Horsfield comes to the belief function. What confronts them now is a string of belief statements equal to the Nicene creed: that the sponsoring system is able to meet all human needs; that the economic order is fundamental and human enjoyment supreme; that success is measured by possessions and power, and happiness is to be found in acquired goods and services; that the world is a violent place and social violence is basically irrational; that there is no greater worth than that a person be young, male and white; that finding easy ways to avoid one's problems is better than struggling through them; that most of life's problems can be solved through buying a product, passing a law or applying a technology. In other words it is giving them, as Bouma would say, a meaning system for life, only this system has the 'wrong' kind of values.

Horsfield points out how this television religion is effecting theology. Instead of God being an object of love and service and gratitude, God now becomes a device to meet one's needs. The question becomes: what can religion do for me? Some modern churches now offer a 'comprehensive religious service' for the mobile client who wants as many needs fulfilled at once as possible.

In my mind there is no doubt that television has a strong enculturation role right from the youngest age and a role of diffusion for the older generations who grew up initially without television. Billions of dollars are spent on television advertising in attempts to change our lifestyles. With a portrayal of violence and sexual exploitation the television gives the impression that these behaviours are acceptable. Coarse language is used so much that it appears the norm. Frequent recourse to themes of pre- and extra-marital sex and the use of drugs gives the impression that these things are normal everyday occurrences. The individual discovers too late that the world of television is not the real world.

There is another negative point worth making. The individual can pick and choose those television messages that reinforce already held attitudes and beliefs. People are literally not able to see and hear others.

One can see the negative side better if one juxtaposes media and gospel values. The media frequently places too much emphasis on providing for the future, in talking about and promoting insurance, superannuation and health cover; it advocates freedom from everyday responsibilities by various forms of escape; it portrays violence as the solution to conflict; it emphasises power as most desirable and projects financial success as the acme of human endeavour; it emphasises material things, self-indulgence, pride, power in the present without any vision of God or life beyond the present one. In contrast to these are the gospel values: the 'good life' includes elements such as honesty, forgiveness, compassion, doing good to others, justice and generosity; God cares for all; we should not be too anxious about the future; money is not everything; humility, love, trust and hope, are worth cultivating; in every life there is the reality of the cross.

Thus in many ways the messages of the media are contrary to Christianity and other religions. But that is not to condemn the media out of hand. What was said above was qualified by saying 'parts of the media' or 'often' or 'too much emphasis'.

Others would say that the churches do not know how to communicate with the public in either the electronic or print media and do not spend the time and money on training their personnel to do so. They have themselves to blame.

Yet others again would say that the medium is impossible for religion, which cannot be 'sold' in thirty second grabs. I will take up this question below. What the above documents do show very clearly is that television often portrays an unreal world emphasising exploitative sex and gratuitous violence. Its values are success, wealth and freedom from responsibility.

We need now to narrow our focus and explore the place of religion in the media before asking the question of how the media treats religion.

The place of religion in the Australian media

Having considered the positive and negative aspects of television, it is time to profile religion in the Australian media. In many ways religion has been marginalised by the Australian media. On radio and television, religious shows are largely excluded from prime time. Even on a Sunday, the TV show, *Compass*, is run after ten o'clock. There seems to be a desire on the part of some to hide religion from public view as much as possible. The low profile of religion in the print media is borne out by the research of Selway who maintains that:

> Religion reporting is considered by most metropolitan daily newspaper establishments as a minor round and religion reporting is usually done in conjunction with two other rounds (for example, education and immigration).[184]

Muriel Porter agrees with Selway claiming that 'the print media has virtually turned its back on religious news in general'.[185] Some in government bureaucracy wanted to do away with the questions on religion in the last census which is indicative of a minority who seem to resent the presence of religion.

What however is on offer? Programs like the American *The Hour of Power* (six am), or *Turn Round Australia* (six am) are evangelical in nature and offered on commercial stations. Channel 10 still provides the worship segment *Mass For You at Home* (six am), while at the other end of the spectrum ABC has *Songs of Praise* at 11am, often followed by another religious program at 11.30am, while *Compass*, which began in 1988, (usually at 10.30pm), treats religious topics in a phenomenological, sociological or comparative way. The times of these religious programs are an indication of the marginalised position that they occupy in the minds of the decision-makers. As regards the future, it has been reported that the Jesuit-backed Lifevision Network could become the first mainstream religion in Australia to join the pay television era by buying two cable television channels on Foxtel.[186]

All news is interpretation

On radio, a comparatively recent initiative was the setting up of the Central Australian Aboriginal Media Association (CAAMA) in 1980. Among other things it offers radio programs that treat of Aboriginal spirituality.[187] The Sydney-based Radio 2GB (once 87 per cent owned by the UCA, now sold off) offered until recently *Sunday Night Live with the Reverend Dr Gordon Moyes*. A Sydney FM station, 2CBA, is an entirely Christian station but of the more fundamentalist kind. For the mainstreamers, however, the ABC offers most in this field. It runs some very professional religious programs which undergo a metamorphosis from time to time reappearing with a new name and format. The ABC has religious programs such as *Come Sunday*, *Encounter*, *Meridian*, *The Word to Say It* (inexplicably replacing, in 1994, the highly acclaimed Caroline Jones program, *Search for Meaning*), and *Religion Today* (formerly The Religion Report), while Classical FM has *For the God who Sings* on Sundays. These programs continue to offer good coverage to listeners on a very broad spectrum of religious affairs. The church historian, Ian Breward, is high in his praise of these programs:

> The ABC is an exception to the way commercial broadcasters have marginalised religion. Its musical, news and commentary programs have played an important role in broadcasting Christian views and helping Christians listen to one another.[188]

Paul Collins, well-known to the public for his criticisms of his own Catholic Church, has shown how the ABC's commitment goes back to 1941 when Kenneth Hendersen, an Anglican minister, was asked to produce programs 'around themes of spiritual morale and post-war reconstruction in the difficult wartime period'.[189] Since then the ABC, both radio and television, has kept up a lively coverage of religion. It has difficulty persuading some sections of the population that the ABC should not be engaged in evangelical broadcasting, and others that it should cover religions other than Christianity.

The ABC does not see itself in the business of promoting Christian beliefs and values. It sees the need to reflect 'an ever-growing plurality' in the religious profile of Australia, according to Hinton.[190] The policy, as far as airtime goes, is to apportion time according to the proportional religious make-up of the Australian population.[191]

Collins is convinced that interest in religion is on the increase in the population. He maintains that religion is becoming 'an increasingly major item on radio talk programs, in current affairs and in specialist output that is characteristic of Radio National'.[192]

The rise in interest in religion is worth elaborating on briefly. It seems to me that the increased interest in religion has many strands to it. We mentioned it when speaking about religion in general and Islam in particular in the *Introduction*. The religions of the East also in recent decades have held fascination for, and given satisfaction to, many westerners, particularly the young. The New Age movement is another strand. The question to be asked is: what are young people searching for and what are they finding in this multifaceted movement? Obviously much that their local denominations are not providing. There is also the strand of dissatisfaction of many westerners with the rampant materialism in our society.

The rise of creation spirituality inspired by the writings of Thomas Berry, Matthew Fox and others has struck a receptive chord in the hearts of many. Creation spirituality has a primal quality that re-unites people with their roots. Hence the popularity of indigenous spiritualities like those of the Cherokee, Navaho, Iroquois, and Sioux of North America and the Aborigines of Australia.

Since the urbanisation of humankind people have been moving progressively further away from the land. What was a slow and gentle trend in medieval Europe, increased with the industrial revolution and has become a galloping nightmare as mega-cities with millions of people cannot stop the exponential growth of urban slums as rural people move into cities in search of work. Not surprisingly the spiritual books that some are reading are the mystical writers of the Rhineland (Hildegaard of Bingen, Mechtild of Magdeburg, Meister Eckhart) who delighted in nature - back in the time just prior to the rise of towns.

Chris McGillion speaks of the new interest in spirituality and how Australians are keen to learn from Aboriginal spirituality.[193] So we are finally beginning to see that they have something to teach us. The writings of Swain, Stockton, Fletcher and others have been catalysts in this regard.

So much for the rising interest in religion. Collins might be picking up this western trend in his radio talkback programs. Now we turn our attention back to the two poles in our discussion, the media and religion.

How does the media treat religion?

Let us now consider how the media treats religion and specifically Christianity. Often it is only if the issues are sensational, controversial, a novelty or somehow capable of a laugh that the media is interested.[194] A prime example of this was the Anglican women's ordination saga which, according to Porter, the media saw as 'a rattling good story'.[195]

Kenneth Woodward, religion editor of *Newsweek*, says the same in an article full of interesting insights on this topic.[196] This applies particularly to the news, commentary on the news, or topical programs. Accounts of alleged healing or Pentecostal services with the use of glossolalia are likely to grab the front page of a daily. Anything to do with Catholic/Private schools, their funding or their performance in public exams (especially if comparisons with Government schools can be made) is worth a run. Moral issues such as the sexual abuse of youngsters by the clergy or others is another example, or Fred Nile (a 'moral crusader' according to the media) interviewed in the hope that his opinions will prove intriguingly outrageous. Ted Kennedy or Ted Noffs as mentioned above, are good copy.

The media often ridicules religion. One is familiar with the stereotype of the ineffectual vicar in many dramas, comedies and advertisements. One thinks too of Homer's pentecostal-type neighbour, Ned Flanders, in the television show *The Simpsons*. In the Australian soap opera *E Street*, the script-writers went overboard in trying to reverse the clerical stereotype by consciously casting the minister of religion as the 'cool' Rev Bob, who wore an earring and rode a motorbike.

Religion does not occur only in sensational contexts. There are the traditional messages (on television or in print) from church leaders at Christmas, the beginning of Lent and Easter. They are strong reminders of the Anglo-Christian origins of the Australian culture and how these origins are still reflected in societal structures today. The *SMH* for example was founded by the Fairfaxes who were devout Christians. Even today anyone born into Australian society will be enculturated into a society with a definite Christian flavour to it.

But there are more serious religious issues that the media finds newsworthy. There is the consistent mention of the welfare work of such agencies as St Vincent de Paul, Lifeline, Care, and World Vision. Suter[197] mentions issues like nuclear disarmament in the 1980s and Armageddon and liberation theology. All these made the headlines but for different reasons. Nuclear disarmament was reported as a church issue because the issue was first raised by the churches in Australia in the context of the newly developed doctrine (in the USA) of limited nuclear warfare. The churches protested against this policy and were the first to bring it to public attention in Australia. Armageddon theology was a goer from the beginning because it is so zany and liberation theology is newsworthy as church business because it has associations with Marxism and, therefore, potentially threatening to capitalistic interests such as media ownership.

One exception to this, are the ABC Television programs such as those mentioned above which do attempt to treat religious issues seriously. The topics chosen are from a broad spectrum of world religions and Christian denominations.

How does the media treat other religions? Islam tends to be portrayed as a religion of extremists. The views of its Lakemba (Sydney) mosque leader, Imam Tajaddine Al-Hillaly, always get a good airing precisely because they are extreme and hence sensational. During the Gulf War, the mimicking of Muslims at prayer by some Australian soldiers on camera and the sharp reaction of the Muslim community in Australia (cited above) did nothing to change the image of Muslims as extremists. The infighting over the site of a mosque in Campbelltown, NSW, some years ago did nothing for Islam and less for Christianity in portraying some very racist views. Again there are some exceptions. More serious shows like the ABC *Lateline* have taken up the issue of what the Koran really teaches as opposed to the popular myths about it. Overall though, the treatment of Islam in the media is less than satisfactory. Ahmed Shboul sums it up as follows:

> ... the image of Muslims seems to suffer from a combination of factors ranging from medieval bigotry, to political ideology, to careless stereotyping.[198]

Shboul would prefer if the media ceased to concentrate on the 'otherness' of Muslims and tried to understand them in socio-economic, cultural and environmental terms rather than always in racial, ethnic and confessional categories.

Hinduism is practically not visible in the media except when something outstanding like the new Temple at Helensburgh, NSW, was opened. Judaism gets a coverage quite out of proportion to its minuscule 0.4 per cent of the population (1991 census) for a number of reasons. One is because of the anti-Jewish violence and the constant reminders of the Holocaust through memorial services or speeches. Another is because the Jews have been in Australia since the arrival of the First Fleet and hence are more integral to Australian culture than either Islam, Hinduism, or Buddhism. That however does not make them immune from inaccurate reporting in the media. Goutman highlights the way the Israeli/Palestinian events in recent times have been a cue for many anti-semites carelessly to equate 'Zionist' with 'Jewish'.[199]

If one observes television generally, one would form the idea that religion is very peripheral to Australian life. Woodward, already quoted, agrees with this. Very few soapies have anything associated with religion in them with the exception of a program like *Home and Away*, to give one example, where the priest plays the role of a very caring and 'cool' minister. The whole question of religion being marginalised is according to Woodward, (speaking more specifically here of the print media) a question of the combination of factors. One is the fact that journalists are on average less 'religious' than a cross-section of the population according to a survey in America quoted by Woodward. (However, in much of the article he is speaking of attitudes in the English-speaking world). Thus the point could be made that some journalists may not be that interested in gathering religious news.

Collins, in the article cited above, laments the dearth of journalists in Australia who have some education in religious matters. Lack of knowledge of the subject means they will shy away from coverage of religious news. Another factor to consider is the process of news-filtering by editors.

Woodward quotes the case of Henry Luce, co-founder and first editor of *Time*, who was a committed Presbyterian, promoted religion in *Time* and gave theologians like Reinhold Niebuhr, Paul Tillich, John Courtney Murray front page coverage. He also gave Billy Graham useful prominence in *Time* at the beginning of his career. Conversely, editors or owners who are not interested in religion will give it scant coverage.

The image of religion on television commercials is another source of distortion. The ministers are usually caricatured and religious rituals presented with a degree of ridicule.

On the other hand, a series like *Brides of Christ*, referred to above, in spite of, or because of, its critical religious content (the trauma of Vatican II for Catholics), caught the public imagination and interest.

The effectiveness of the religious media

So much for where religion stands in the Australian media and how it is treated. Now let us consider the question of how effective religious programs are. Caution needs to precede financial outlay. The short answer is that no-one quite knows the effect of religious programming. Nichols, writing in 1972, said that he believed that mass communication usually would not produce major behavioural change.[200] It could be the trigger point for a response to the gospel. However, it could be used by the churches to inform people about religious matters. Another writer, Fore, gives much space to research on this topic in his book of 1994. In 1971, *The Pastoral Instruction* was at least aware of this grey area:

> ...... it appears necessary to discover through scientific research the true effectiveness of the Church in the field of social communications. It will then be possible to deploy her resources so that they suit the importance of the tasks she faces throughout the world (art 185).[201]

Perhaps the whole question of the influence of religious programming on television will be seen better in context if we briefly overview the history of television and religion, at least in some countries.

When television first became available, people didn't know how to cope with this new medium. In Britain, for example, when television was introduced there was much debate over religion and its place. At one stage, the television stations were off the air between 6.15pm and 7.30pm so that they would not prevent people from going to church!

In the USA religion used to get some free time on regular television stations but then the private stations started up, often with individual evangelists, with their own money. They soon eclipsed the other religious programs, which could not compete financially. One exception was the program of the Catholic bishop, Fulton J Sheen.

As the private religious stations grew in the 1970s, they became renowned through the names of people like, Billy Graham, Robert Schuller, Rex Humbard, Jim Bakker, Jimmy Swaggart, Pat Robertson, Kenneth

Copeland and Oral Roberts.[202] Constant mail responses and money donations soon made these preachers prisoners to their huge audiences. But they grew in popularity peaking in 1977, according to research, with a weekly audience of 3.9 million for Oral Roberts.

In becoming big business, their agenda became set by their audiences rather than by the gospel. In the 1980s and 1990s we witnssed how some of these evangelists crashed to their ruin through scandals.

How, then, would one evaluate this modern phenomenon of the electronic church? The influence of these electronic churches has been researched and according to Fore it can be summarised as follows:

> ...the electronic church helps some people but misleads far more, and that in the long run it probably is doing more harm than good.[203]

"It's CNN - They want exclusive broadcasting rights to the second coming."

The Electronic church can be misleading.

One of the negative things about the electronic church is that it promotes a very narrow kind of religion, a distorted worldview and has no ecumenical or interfaith dimension. Indeed it is antithetical to the values of toleration if not mutual acceptance and respect required by our modern, global, multifaith village. Interestingly enough these churches have adopted the values of the secular programs with their emphasis on wealth, success, glamour and razzamattazz.[204] One can say televangelism has been devoured by the values of its sponsoring parent, television, yet nevertheless it remains a threat to mainline churches who neglect their parishioners.

Australia has been one the fastest countries in the world to adapt to television. According to Horsfield 'in just three years half the houses in Sydney and Melbourne had their own television sets.'[205] Today more than ninety per cent have.

As regards the relationship between the churches and the media, it is obvious that it is not always a comfortable one. In 1972 Nichols commented that the Anglicans, Methodists and the Salvation Army received the best coverage from the media.[206] The reasons for this were that:

- the *Anglicans* were one of the first into the whole area of media relations, in which they had a highly developed operation by 1972.

- the *Methodists* owed their high profile to the work of Rev Alan Walker at the Central Methodist Mission and their traditional emphasis on social concern. In addition there was the popularity of the Rev Roger Bush on 2GB. (*The Catholics had 2SM but sold it in 1992; 2CH belongs to the NSW Council of Churches.*)

- the *Salvation Army's* popularity dates back to before World War II, and in addition it had a Public Relations unit capitalising on their high standing in the community.

More than twenty years later, one would have to say that sects have a high media profile due to their often bizarre actions, the Anglicans because of the ordination of women and the Catholics in the nineties because of the beatification of Mary MacKillop, the frequent comments of John Paul II and the sexual abuse cases against clergy and members of religious orders.

Often individuals bring their denomination into the news. I am thinking of the late Ted Noffs (UCA) and his work for the homeless and drug addicts, or Ted Kennedy (Catholic) and his social concern for Aborigines. There are other examples. One of the first persons to utilise the television was Rev Alan Walker, well-known as the superintendent of Sydney's Central Methodist Mission. In 1958 he began the television show, *I Challenge the Minister*, on Channel Nine. The format of the program was that Walker would go to any public place or factory and respond to any questions people might wish to ask him. It was a great success, running until 1965, and still holds the record for the highest rating for any religious program.[207]

That Walker was prepared to allow the sharp edge of prophecy to challenge the culture of the times is shown by his preaching against the Vietnam war on 2CH in spite of warnings to him by Canon Broughton Knox, chairman of the NSW Council of Churches (which body held the licence for the station).

Walker's media prominence through his clearly defined position is paralleled in the USA where, according to Woodward, the liberal Protestant churches receive little coverage because of their perceived greyness on issues, whereas the Catholics and the evangelical-fundamentalist movements receive top media coverage.[208]

Having attempted in the above pages to identify what the media is, we reflected on its positive and negative aspects and then tried to narrow our focus by describing religion's place in the media and the way it is treated. This leads us to a position where one can ask: what exactly is the challenge to which the churches, as the visible, public face of religion, are called upon to respond?

The challenge

The real challenge to the churches seems to me to be:

1. can they accept the fact that the modern media, and television in particular, is a different form of communication?

2. can they adapt to this different kind of communication culture? Can they inculturate the gospel message into the modern media?

The Catholic Church sees it optimistically as an opportunity not to be missed.[209] Article 15 of the Vatican II *Decree on the Means of Social Communication* develops the point and states that 'Priests, religious and laity should be trained *at once*' (italics added) to meet the needs described in article 3. That was in 1963! I think Fr Bill Uren, the former leader of the Jesuits in Australia, hit the nail on the head when, talking to a journalist, Peter Fray, he pointed out that 'the church on the whole tends to be a bit frightened of the media. I think it is important we befriend the media and meet it on (its) own terms.'[210]

The question of being a bit afraid of the media needs further exploring. The essence of the problem seems to be that there is a clash of two cultures: (Christian) church culture and Australian media culture. The two do not get on well together. Chris McGillion is of the opinion that basically the cultures are different and that is why so little is reported[211]; he is not proposing change particularly but trying to explain why. He quotes a survey done by Vanderbilt University's Freedom Forum First Amendment Centre which reported that there was a big gap between media and religious culture and that no prejudice on the part of the journalists against religion - it was simply that they did not think religion was newsworthy. Many of the journalists had their own religious beliefs.

Religion gets a bad press because it gets so little press. He contrasts it to sport which is dramatic, emotional, full of conflicts, myths, arguments and heroes. Religion seems dead by comparison with its creeds, codes, exhortations and pious platitudes. It is only when the religious story has some of these qualities that it makes it into the news. Witness the ordination of women issue which is a rattling good story, with conflict (females versus male hierarchy), high emotion (demonstrations, interviews) and impassioned arguments (synods, symposiums, conferences). Another case where religion gets good coverage is in Latin and South America where the Church becomes involved in justice issues. The slaying of Oscar Romero in a packed cathedral in San Salvador comes to mind as just one incident.

Perhaps this last idea lies at the basis of the problem: the Church is too often seen as politically anemic which is ironic in that Jesus was charged with sedition. The Church sees its role as one of moral teaching not political leadership. By political I mean politics in the broad sense not party-politics. If the Church is to be concerned with social transformation, involvement in the political sphere is needed. We have quoted Mannix, MacKillop, Chisholm, Lang, as examples of this. Brian Gore[212] in the Philippines and Alan Walker are more recent examples. McGillion also refers to the Southern Baptists in the States and the way they developed a non-violence movement directing mass action against racial discrimination. That produced results in the long run. McGillion concludes, '... a church that does not take social justice seriously enough to fight for it may be many things but it is not faithful to the gospel of Jesus Christ'.[213] Perhaps if it did it would be seen to be more involved in the blood and guts issues of life and hence be worth reporting. Indeed the Church is a bit afraid of the media because it does not understand it and wants to present a face to the media that might not be worth reporting.

Writing in 1993, John Coleman in the editorial of *Concilium*[214] formulates one of the questions that must be addressed as 'What does the Church need to know about the media to negotiate its use and to fulfil its mission of discernment about modern culture?' The answers have been slow in coming. In 1993 the questions were still being asked! Selway argues for media workshops for 'religious groups' with the purpose of building up understanding and trust (so often lacking) between the media and religious groups.[215]

Decrees, being statements are limited in what they can do. However Vatican II did decide to do two things. Firstly, to set aside one day each year (Social Communication Sunday, now World Communications Day) to raise people's consciousness of the media, or as the decree says, to remind all 'of their duties in this domain' (art 18). Secondly, the Council 'decided and ordained that national offices for the press, the cinema, radio and television be established everywhere and be properly supported.' Presumably the support intended was mainly of a financial nature. It would be interesting to know how many of these initiatives limp for lack of financial support. In the USA this led to the Catholic Conference establishing an Office of Radio and Television in 1968 to represent it in all broadcasting matters. The equivalent occurred in Sydney, in 1960 with the title of 'Catholic Communications', then became 'The Catholic Audio/Visual Centre' and now is known as 'The Catholic Communications Centre'.

It was resolved by the Council also that another, more complete treatment of the media be undertaken once the Council was over. This resulted in another document published by the Pontifical Commission for the Means of Social Communication on 29 January 1971, called *Pastoral Instruction on the Means of Social Communication*, referred to above. This document shows that the Church does not know yet quite how to use the media. It is alert to the fact that different skills are required by different media and that the mode of presentation has to suit the nature of the medium. Where the Church makes programs, the standard should be at least as good as secular ones. Not surprisingly the document ends with the less than contentious comment that 'more study needs to be done on the media' (art 184).

Some historical insight into what has happened in the relationship and power struggle between church and society will help to situate the present issues in a meaningful framework. Up to the Middle Ages, when manuscripts reigned supreme, the literate clergy and theologians held enormous power over the illiterate. The oral word was the commonest means of communication and listening to a good preacher was a social as much as a religious occasion. In the sixteenth century, Gutenberg's printing press put the bible into people's hands and the printed word progressively became the main means of communication.

Now we are into the electronic era. As Marshal McLuhan hyperbolically stated: the medium is the message. Images and sound are used to get messages across. It is like a ritual act whereby the believer is 'tirelessly conquering the world, organising it, transforming the landscape of nature into a cultural milieu.'[216] Television does this. It transforms reality into its own images, its own values, its own milieu and thus creates its own culture.

The role of the churches is one of 'Christ and culture in paradox' and 'Christ transforming culture' to use Niebuhr's terms[217]. That is, the Christian Church has to be countercultural where the values of society contradict the gospel values, and on other occasions, it plays the role of transforming what it finds in society, that is, it builds and transforms something that is good or potentially so.

Fore expresses the role as follows:

It requires of the church that it supply the critical tools and context for the unmasking, which means that the images of television must become part of the sermonic and teaching elements of the church environment.[218]

With the 'critical tools' goes the concept of negotiated meaning. It is not enough simply to watch programs and take what one wills from them. The task of processing the content with others or alone must be encouraged with these critical tools (objectives of the producer, strategies used to achieve them, evidence, bias, values promoted, sponsoring bodies, etc.) so that some parts of the program are accepted, others rejected, other evidence considered, and finally a 'negotiated meaning' given to the program which may be quite different from what the producer had in mind.

The churches can play a positive role in the media in general by assisting programmers, particularly in matters of religion. Matters of religion are included implicitly or explicitly in general broadcasting. As Fuchs points out:

> More attention will be paid to such forms of the presence of religion in the media if the media are not used as instruments for church interests but there is co-operation with those who work as producers and artists in a way which builds up relationships that bring mutual recognition and enrichment.[219]

Religion has to be aware of this kind of culture when it tries to relate to the electronic media. Television has severe limitations. Some, including Karl Rahner and Johann Metz, would say that there are certain religious programs that should never be televised, such as the Eucharistic celebration.[220] The reason for this is that the sacred place and time required for this celebration cannot be guaranteed. However, this opinion has lost out in many quarters as is seen, for example, in the fact of Sunday *Worship* on ABC or the fact that the papal eucharistic celebrations continue to be televised, as was the case with the beatification of Mary MacKillop at Randwick Racecourse in January 1995.

Television is about the quick thirty-second grab, not about metaphysical debates. It is not geared for subtle discourse. This is illustrated strikingly in an article by Russo in which he shows how three different American

archbishops, Bernardin, O'Connor and Weakland han-
dled the tricky issue of abortion and how the media
finally reported them.[221] The print media has similar
problems, as Bentley has shown in an article on the
reporting of the *SMH* on the Seventh-Day Adventists.[222]
The media, conscious of its audiences, either does not
have the time for the many nuances or details that
such complicated subjects as abortion or the Seventh-
Day Adventists demand for accurate reporting, or is
not able to overcome its prejudice when reporting such
matters.

When religious programs report on religion, they
must be aware that ultimately they are there 'to help
people interpret their existence in the light of what
God has done for them as manifest in Jesus Christ'.[223]
Nichols supports the idea that the positive aspects of
Christianity should be brought out on television.[224] The
critical point, as Fore says, is not to present the gospel *so*
that people accept it, but to present it *so well* that they
can accept it.

Religious television must now find ways of telling its
stories, as Morris points out. It must use testimonies,
news, biographies, documentaries, worship and drama
(witness the success of the ABC drama, *Brides of Christ*,
or *Mary MacKillop*). Babin agrees, recommending the
use of 'the Christian happenings, the history of our her-
itage and parables, stories and testimonies'.[225] If it refus-
es to do so, it will forfeit the use of a very powerful
medium of communication.

Time and money are needed to provide for better
programming which incorporates gospel values. Many
television programs are produced in a rushed way without considering values. Often writers know that sex and
violence are part of a recipe that will attract some audi-

ences. The Jesuits are planning to remedy the sex-and-violence menu through Lifevision which plans to broadcast up to sixteen hours a day documentaries, news, films, other family entertainment, youth culture, motherhood, ecology and spiritual matters.[226] But over and above the Jesuit initiative, talented people are needed to write more constructive and more thoughtful material for programs in general. It might take more time and money, but it is necessary if we want to provide an alternative to quick, superficial programs frequently focused on exploitative sex and gratuitous violence. These programs which may be produced by the churches or in collaboration with others, would have as their overall aim,

... to illuminate the human condition, to ask meaningful religious questions, to rediscover religious truths, and to find new religious vocabulary which can have meaning and power for multitudes of men and women today.[227]

Are the churches prepared to support this thrust with money?

Summary

The media is all the electronic and print ways used to communicate within and with society. The church documents and other writings of experts have given us a solid appreciation of the many positive values of the media such as providing companionship, entertainment, information and promoting the unity of all humankind. Negatively, the media often portrays an unreal world emphasising exploitative sex and gratuitous violence. Its values are success, wealth and freedom from responsibility.

Looking at the reality in Australia, the media generally marginalises religion, the ABC being one notable exception. The churches have said much of value about the media on a theoretical level but have shown little practical understanding in relating to the media. Since church culture and media culture are very different, the challenge for churches is to try to understand the media culture; to do something regarding the training of personnel to relate effectively to the media; to avoid the trap that televangelism has fallen into; to develop good quality religious programs (as some already do) and to co-operate as fully as possible with general programs.

Points to ponder:

1. How are love and sex portrayed on some television programs you may have seen?

2. Which values on the media would you consider anti-gospel?

3. Is watching worship on television essentially different from attending in person? Explain your answer.

4. What topics should religious television programs cover as opposed to radio?

5. Is there a place for evangelical-type programs on television?

6. What avenues of communication on television should the Christian churches in Australia explore?

7. People, especially the young, should take care to develop moderation and self-control in the use of these instruments. Their goal should be an ever more discerning grasp of what they see, hear, and read. Discussions with educators and appropriate experts will school them to make mature judgments. (# 10 *Decree on the Means of Social Communication*, Vatican II document, 1963.)

Do you agree with this statement? How do people today gain discernment regarding the media?

Glossary

acculturation: the process whereby major cultural changes occur, sometimes by duress, as a result of prolonged contact between societies.

animatism: a belief that the world is animated by impersonal supernatural powers, e.g., the *mana* in Melanesia.

animism: a belief in spirit beings thought to animate nature.

anthropology: from the Greek, *anthropos*, human being and *logos*, study; the study of human beings.

beliefs: snapshots of theology relating to individual teachings. A belief is a formulation of the knowledge we have of God through faith.

cultural anthropology: the study that describes the forms of social organisation and the cultural systems of human groups.

culture: the sum total of a way of life of a given group of people including artefacts, behaviour and meanings underpinning these.

diachronic: relating to a study or observation of a phenomenon over time.

diffusion(ism): the theory that customs, practices or items of culture spread from one culture to another.

emic(ly): from the word *phonemic*, applied to studying a culture from the inside, without preconceived categories of meaning.

enculturation: the process whereby individuals learn their culture; it occurs only once in a lifetime.

ethnocentrism: the tendency to focus on one's own culture to the exclusion of others; to see one's own culture as the best and the standard for all others.

ethnography: the study that describes the social and cultural systems of one particular group.

ethnology: the comparison of ethnographic studies for the purpose of generalising about the nature of all human groups.

etic(ly): from the word, *phonetic*; applied to the study of a culture from the outside according to preconceived ideas of phonology and grammar.

etiology: the phenomenon whereby existing situations are explained by way of a story alleged to have happened in the past.

evolution: the theory that culture progressed through stages from the primal to the civilised.

faith: a word frequently found in the same context as religion. It can have many different shades of meanings. *Religious* faith is belief and trust in gods, or a God, or an all-pervasive power.

functionalism: the theory that sought to explain cultural customs in terms of their function in a society.

inculturation: the dynamic and critically interactive relation between the Christian message and culture or cultures; an insertion of the Christian life into a culture; an ongoing process of reciprocal and critical interaction and assimilation between them.

magisterium: the teaching authority of the Catholic Church located in the pope and bishops.

magic: the belief that supernatural powers can be manipulated for good or evil by the use of certain formulas.

modernity: the resulting characteristics of the process of modernisation in individuals, institutions, countries and cultures.

modernisation: the process of transformation of the world as a result of increasing knowledge dynamically translated into technology.

monocultural: relating to one culture only. A society can be monocultural if only one culture is present.

monogenism: the theory that all humankind came from a single couple, (the opposite to polygenism).

multicultural: consisting of many ethnic or cultural groups.

multiculturalism: the state of having many cultures; as a policy it is the attitude of positively accepting different cultures in a society.

native exegesis: the explanation of a culture by someone inside the culture.

neo-evolutionism: a later form of evolutionism.

origination: applied to changes that arise from within the culture itself.

persistence: the continuance of cultural items, practices or customs which can be (i) general, (pervades all the culture), (ii) sectional (only certain aspects of a culture), or (iii) partial (a custom carried out with reduced frequency).

polyethnic: consisting of many ethnic or cultural groups.

polygenism: the theory that human beings descended from several members of a first human generation.

relativism (cultural): the idea that because cultures are unique, they can be evaluated only according to their own standards and not by any outside values. (The opposite to ethnocentricism).

religion: the system of beliefs and practices whereby people come to terms with ultimate realities.

religious tradition: can mean *world religion*, as in the expression, the 'major religious traditions of the world'. It can also mean a *Christian church or denomination*, such as 'the different religious traditions in Christianity, like the Greek Orthodox, Baptists and the Presbyterians'. It can also mean a rite in the Catholic Church, such as 'there are many different religious traditions in the Catholic Church such as the Maronites, Ukrainians and Melchites'. The religious composition of Australia today allows for all three uses.

sectarianism: an attitude of dislike or hatred towards Christian churches other than one's own.

secular: relating to this world as opposed to 'religious' things.

secularism: a vision of life that explains all in terms of this material world to the exclusion of God.

secularisation: the vision of life in which all areas have their respective autonomy as opposed to a vision of reality that sees all aspects of life as immediately explained in religious terms.

society: a permanent organised aggregate of persons sharing a common way of life and group consciousness.

stereotype: a way of seeing and describing something or someone which is not true to reality but has become the conventional and prejudiced way.

structural-functionalism: a modified form of functionalism which maintained that each custom and belief had a specific function that served to perpetuate the structure of that society.

structuralism: the theory that sees the components of culture, especially myth, as having meaning and inter-related and supporting each other; it allows myth to speak without imposing a meaning on it.

subculture: a society may include a number of subgroups or subcultures; a subculture is a group which is partly dependent and partly independent of the large unit, the society.

survivals: elements of a culture that have, with the passage of time, changed their function and become mere conventions.

symbiosis: the process of mutual interaction and mutual influence of two forces; the individual and the group are said to be in a symbiotic relationship as regards cultural influence.

synchronic: relating to a study of some phenomenon across different situations and cultures at the same point of time in history.

theology: the scientific study of faith in order to reach greater understanding thereof; 'faith seeking understanding'.

transcultural: refers to the transference of cultural elements of a specific culture to almost all other cultures while resisting their influence upon itself.

universal: a pattern that is basic to human nature and common to all societies.

witchcraft: occurs when a misfortune such as sickness or death, is attributed to the innate, psychic powers allegedly possessed by some individuals.

world religions: the five (major), world religions (in alphabetical order) Buddhism, Christianity, Hinduism, Islam, and Judaism, and lesser known religions and others called tribal or primal religions.

Notes

Introduction

1. Paul Collins, *God's Earth: Religion as if matter really mattered*, Melbourne: Dove, 1995.

2. Towns in NSW with a high Aboriginal population and high unemployment.

3. This refers to a controversial project to build a bridge in SA over land alleged to be sacred to the Aborigines.

4. Although 'media' is technically plural in meaning, I will use it grammatically as singular.

5. D.Horne, 'The Great Celtic Con Job', *The Sydney Morning Herald* (hereafter *SMH*), 2 September 1995, Spectrum 7A.

1. What is culture?

6. C. Geertz, *The Interpretation of Cultures*, London, Fontana Press, 1973, 34-39.

7. Pius XII's encyclical, *Humani Generis* where he says of polygenism that it is difficult to see how it can be reconciled with the teaching on original sin.

8. E. Hoebel, and T. Weaver, *Anthropology and The Human Experience*, 5th ed., New York: McGraw-Hill Book Company, 1979, 289.

9. Louis Luzbetak, *The Church and Cultures:* An Applied Anthropology for the Religious Worker, William Carey Library, Techny, Illinois: The Divine Word Publications, 1970, 12.

10. Robert Schreiter, *Constructing Local Theologies*, New York: Orbis Books, 1982, 41.

11. R. Beals, H. Hoijer, and A. Beals, An Introduction to Anthropology, 5th ed. New York: MacMillan, 1977, 130.

12. ibid. 119, 120.

13. C. Geertz, *Interpretation*, 35.

14. ibid.

15. Bronislaw Malinowski, *Argonauts of the Western Pacific*, London: Routledge and Keagan Paul Ltd., 1922.

16. Alfred Radcliffe-Brown, *The Andaman Islanders*, CUP, 1922.

17. Included in this is the concept of the new ethnography which encourages the emic (from phonemic, meaning 'from the inside'), and opposed to etic, (from phonetic, meaning 'from the outside') study of culture i.e, without any preconceived or absolute cognitive categories. cf. Louis Luzbetak, *The Church and Cultures: New Perspectives in missiological anthropology*, Maryknoll: Orbis Books, 1988:150. I am focusing on the Anglo-American group. The French school of Barthes, de Saussure and Levi-Strauss and the Russian school of Tortu and Lotman are acknowledged but need not concern us directly here.

18. C.Geertz, *Interpretation*, 5.

19. Karl Marx, 'Preface', in *A Contribution to the Critique of Political Economy*, 1923, New York: International, 1970, quoted in W. Roseberry, *Anthropologies and Histories: essays in culture, history and political economy*, New Brunswick: Rutgers University Press, 1991: 37.

212 • RELIGION IN AUSTRALIAN CULTURE

20. A. Williams, *Marxism and Literature*, Oxford: OUP, 1977, quoted in Rosebery, ibid. 45.

21. E.B. Tylor, *Primitive Culture: Researchers into the Development of Mythology, Philosophy, Religion, Language, Art and Customs*, vols, 1-2, London: John Murray, 1903 [1871]: 1.

22. cf. F. Boas, 'Anthropology', in *Encyclopedia of the Social Sciences*, vol.2, New York: The McMillan Company, 1930: 79. quoted in A.Darcy, 'Franz Boas and the concept of culture: a genealogy', in *Creating Culture*, Austin-Broos, D, ed., Sydney: Allen and Unwin, 1987: 5.

23. R. Lowie, *The History of Ethnological Theory*, New York: Rhinehart, 137: 3, quoted in Luzbetak, *New Perspectives*, 60.

24. W. Haviland, *Cultural Anthropology*, New York: Holt, Rinehart and Winston, 6th ed.,1978: 29.

25. Austin-Roos, *Creating*, x.

26. C. Geertz, *Interpretation*, page 6

27. L. Luzbetak, *An Applied Anthropology*, 172. Examples are B.Malinowski and R.Piddington.

28. ibid., 176.

29. ibid., 178.

2. How is culture acquired?

30. An ecumenical movement named after the place where it started in France. It is noted for its distinctive style of prayer and singing.

31. R.Ward, *Australia, A Short History*, Sydney: Ure Smith, 1975: 102.

32. M. Azevedo, *Inculturation and the Challenges of Modernity*, Rome: Centre 'Cultures and Religion'- Pontifical Gregorian Univeristy, 1982, 4.

33. ibid., 11.

34. L. Luzbetak, *An Applied Anthropology*, 73,74.

35. J. Harris, One Blood: *200 Years of Aboriginal Encounter with Christianity A Story of Hope*, Sutherland:Albatross, 1990, 105.

36. L. Luzbetak, *An Applied Anthroplogy*, 93.

37. ibid. ,143,144.

38. E. Stockton, *The Aboriginal Gift: Spirituality for a Nation*, Alexandria, Sydney: Millennium, 1995: 14; T. Swain, quoting the art work of northern Australia, says at least 60 000 years, cf. *A Place for Strangers*, CUP, 1993, 5.

39. L. Luzbetak, *New Perspectives*, 143.

40. T. Swain, *A Place*, 120.

41. Anthony Kelly, 'Theology in an Australian Context', *Compass* 12 no 2, Winter 1978: 1-7.

42. Hugh Mackay, *Reinventing Australia: The mind and mood of Australia in the 90s*, Sydney: Angus and Robertson, 1993.

43. ibid., 61.

44. Moira Eastman, *Family, the vital factor: the key to society's survival*, Blackburn: Collins Dove, 1989.

45. Veronica Brady, *SMH*, 29 January 1994, p.9A

46. T. Swain, *A Place*.

47. M. Azevedo, *Inculturation*, 46.

48. J.Metz, *Faith in History and Society: Towards a Practical Fundamental Theology*, London: Burns and Oates, 1980, 169.

3. What is religion?

49. P. Meagher, ed., *Encyclopedic Dictionary of Religion*, vol.3 (0-Z), Washington: Corpus Publications, 1979, 3005-3009.

50. Gary Bouma, *Religion: Meaning, transcendence and community in Australia*, Melbourne: Longman Cheshire, 1992, Chapter 1.

51. N. Habel and B. Moore, *When Religion Goes to School*, Adelaide: South Australia College of Advanced Education, 1982, 8-21.

52. Quoted in Karl Barth, *The Epistle to the Romans*, trans. E.C.Hoskyns London: OUP, 1968, 258.

53. Rudolf Otto, *The Idea of the Holy*, London: Oxford University Press, 1969.

54. Ninian Smart, *The Religious Experience of Mankind*, New York: Collins, 1971, 15-25.

55. G. Bouma, *Religion*, 75.

56. K. Barth, *Epistle*, 47.

57. ibid., 129.

58 Karl Barth, *Church Dogmatics, vol.1, The Doctrine of the Word of God: Prolegomena to Church Dogmatics*, Part 2, Edinburgh: T & T Clark, 1970, 185. The topic is treated in Part III, par. 17: The Revelation of God as the Abolition of Religion, 280-361.

59. ibid., 190.

60. ibid., 236.

61. ibid., 238.

62. ibid., 230.

63. ibid., 280.

64. ibid., 231.

65 ibid., 325,326.

66. ibid., 293.

67. ibid., 281.

68. C. Geertz, *Interpretation*, 99.

69. B. Malinowski, *Magic*, 67.

70. ibid., 24.

71. B. Malinowski, *Other Essays*.

72. M.Bloch, *Prey into hunter*, Cambridge Univeristy Press,1992, 99-100.

73. C. Geertz, *Interpretation*, 103.

74. ibid., 87-125.

75. ibid., 87.

76. ibid., 88.

77. W. Haviland, *Cultural*, 355.

4. Imposing Anglo-Celtic culture

78. According to the latest rock art findings at Jinmium, Northern Territory, by Dr Richard Fullagar, possibly 175 000 years ago, cf.*SMH*, 21 September 1996, p.29

79. P. Grimshaw, et al, *Creating a Nation*, Ringwood, McPheeGribble, 1994, 137. Estimates of the number of Aborigines vary. Price gives 314 500 C.Price, 'Immigration and Ethnic Origin', in *Australians: Historical Statistics*, ed. W.Vamplew, Sydney: Fairfax, Syme and Weldon Associates, 1987, 4.; Eugene Stockton, *The Aboriginal Gift, Spirituality for a Nation*, Sydney: EJ Dwyer, 1995, 25.) comments that the figure originally thought to be 300 000 has now been revised upwards to between 750 000 and 1 million.

80. Quoted in M. Hogan, *The Sectarian Strand: Religion in Australian history*, Ringwood: Pengiun,1987, 15, 16.

81. Quoted in H. Reynolds, *Frontier, Aborigines, Settlers and Land*, Sydney: Allen and Unwin, 1987, 108.

82. J.Bickford, *Christian Work in Australia*, London: Wesleyan Conference, 1878, 29-30, quoted in I. Breward, *A History of the Australian Churches*, Sydney: Allen and Unwin, 1993, 2.

83. J. Harris, *One Blood*, 29.

84. I. Breward, *History*, 15.

85. C.Smith, *The Booandik Tribe of South Australian Aborigines*, North Terrace: E.Spiller, 1880, quoted in T. Swain, *Interprreting Aborignal Religion: An Historical Account*, Bedford Park: Australian Association for the Study of Religion, 1985, 24.

86. J. Harris, *One Blood*, 46.

87. H. Nelson, 1965, 'The Missionaries and the Aborigines in the Port Phillip District', *Historical Studies*, 12 (1965): 57-60, quoted in Swain, *Interpreting*, 135, note 4.

88. J. Harris, *One Blood*, 47.

89. M. Hogan, *Sectarian*, 17.

90. E. Stockton, *Gift*, 52.

91. B. Malinowski, *Other Essays*, 23.

92. H. Reynolds, 'The Rights of the Land', *Frontier, Aborigines, Settlers and Land*, Sydney: Allen and Unwin, 1987, 133-161.

93. The ABC TV program, on *Multiculturalism in Australia*. Mary Kalantzis lectured at that time, in the Centre for Multicultural Studies at Wollongong University.

94. P. Robinson, *The Hatch and Brood of Time: A Study of the first generation of native-born white Australians 1788-1828*, Melbourne: UOP, 1985; and *The Women of Botany Bay: An Interpretation of the role of women in the origins of Australian society*, Ringwood: Penguin Books, 1993.

95. J. Harris, *One Blood*, 60.

96. H. Reynolds, *The Other Side of the Frontier*, Ringwood: Pengiun Books, 1981, 189.

97 J. Harris, *One Blood*, 72.

98. *The Sunday Telegraph,* 29 October, 1972, quoted in R. Ward's, *Australia: A Short History,* Sydney: Ure Smith, 1975, 192.

99. H. Reynolds, *The Other Side,* 192.

100. ibid., 61,62.

101. M. Hogan, *Sectarian,* 71.

102. E. Stockton, *Gift* , 7.

103. Dom Salvado (1814-1900) was a Benedictine monk who founded, in 1846, a monastery and village at New Norcia in WA as a mission for Aborigines.

104. A. Grocott, *Convicts, clergymen and churches: attitudes of convicts and ex-convicts towards the churches and religion,* Sydney: Sydney University Press, 1980, 57.

105. P. Grimshaw, *Creating,* 80.

106. I. Breward, *History,* 92.

107. W. Vamplew, ed. *Australians,* 10: 421.

108. A group of Irish convicts from Castle Hill near Sydney, unsuccessfully rose up against the British in 1804 at a place called Vinegar Hill.

109. B. Malinowski, *Other Essays,* 84.

110. M. McKernan, *Australian Churches at War,* Sydney: Catholic Theological Faculty, St Patrick's Manly and the Australian War Memorial, 1980, 18,19.

111. A. Grocott, *Convicts,* 279.

112. J. Molony, *History of Australia: The Story of 200 Years,* Ringwood: Viking, 1987, 61.

113. Patrick O'Farrell, *The Catholic Church and Community in Australia,* Melbourne, Nelson, 1977, 184; Later another Pope, Pius XI, further supported this emphasis on Catholic schools with his encyclical, *Divini illius magistri* of 31 December, 1929.

114. In 1995 the schools in Melbourne and Sydney were $20 million in debt. The Jewish community pledged to pay their way out of the mess. cf. *SMH,* 4 February 1995, p.8.

115. P. O'Farrell, *Church,* 185.

116. ibid., 39.

117. M. Hogan. *Sectarian,* 10.

118. J.D. Bollen, *Protestantism and Social Reform in New South Wales 1890-1910,* Melbourne: Melbourne University Press, 1972, 144.

119. J. Molony, *Story,* 70.

120. P. Grimshaw, *Creating,* 157.

121. M. Hogan, *Sectarian,* 75.

122. Ian Gillman, ed. *Many Faiths One Nation,* Sydney: Collins Australia, 1988, 277.

123. I. Breward, *History,* 101.

124. ibid., 85,86.

125. D. Wright, and E. Clancy, *The Methodists: A History of Methodism in NSW,* Sydney: Allen and Unwin, 1993, 44.

126. ibid., 101.

127. A term coined by the American feminist writer Elisabeth Schüssler Fiorenza; it derives from the Greek 'kyrios', Lord, hence meaning 'lordship'.

128. E.Campion, *Rockchoppers*, Ringwood: Penguin, 1982, 44, 45.

129. ibid., 27.

130. Daniel Mannix (1864 - 1963) was Archbishop of the Catholic Archdiocese of Melbourne.

131. ibid., 95.

132. J. Molony, *Story*, 61.

133. D. Wright, *Methodists*, 101.

134. J. Molony, *The Roman Mould of the Australian Catholic Church*, Carlton: Melbourne University Press, 1969.

5. Change, acculturation and persistence in the twentieth century

135. Daniel Mannix, an Irishman, was Catholic Archbishop of Melbourne from 1917-1963 . He was often a very controversial figure.

136. M. Gilchrist, *Daniel Mannix: Priest and Patriot*, Blackburn: Dove Communications, 1982, 101.

137. ibid., 26.

138. ibid., 49.

139. ibid., 71.

140. M. McKernan, *At War*, 64.

141. M. Gilchrist, *Mannix*, 12.

142. J.Moloney, *The Roman Mould of the Australian Catholic Church*, Carlton: Melbourne University Press, 1969.

143. ibid., 62.

144. Frank Engel, *Australian Christians in Conflict and Unity*, 1825-1926, Melbourne: Joint Board of Christian Education of Australia and New Zealand, 1984, and *Christians in Australia, Times of Change 1918-1978*, Melbourne: The Joint Board of Christian Education of Australia and New Zealand, Melbourne, 1993.

145. M. McKernan, *At War*, 139.

146. Argus, 29 May 1939, quoted in B. Santamaria, *Santamaria, Against the Tide*, Melbourne: Oxford University Press, 1981, 41.

147. M. Gilchrist, *Mannix*, 21.

148. B. Santamaria, *Tide*, 95.

149. I. Breward, *History*, 123.

150. D. Wright, *Methodists*, 107. The Methodist were initially strong supporters of the Labor party but soon after its formation withdrew as they saw that Labor did not support their campaign for the observance of the sabbath and against drink and gambling.

151. J. Molony, *Story*, 170.

152. B.Duncan, '40 Years after the s.p.l.i.t.', *National Outlook*, vol.16, no 10, December 1994, 16-19.

153. C. Hally, 'Growth Patterns in the Catholic Church', *The Shape of Belief:*

Christianity in Australia Today, ed. D.Harris et al, Homebush: Lancer, 1982, 85.

154. Peter Kaldor, *Who Goes Where? Who Doesn't Care?*, Sydney: Lancer, 1987.

155. M. Azevedo, *Inculturation*, 19.

156. ibid., 18.

157. D. Walker, 'Models of Spirituality for Ordained Ministers *'Priesthood: The Hard Questions*, Newtown: E J Dwyer, 1993.

158. C. Hally, 'Growth Patterns in the Catholic Church', *The Shape of Belief: Christianity in Australia Today*, eds. D.Harris et al, Homebush, Lancer, 1982, p.78

159. Frank Brennan is an Australian Jesuit and lawyer who has been very active in the defence of Aboriginal rights.

160. ibid., 2.

161. I. Breward, *History*, 122.

162. ibid. 187.

163. *The Catholic Weekly*, 23 March,1994, p 8.

164. Jennifer Corkhill, 'The Ordination of Women: A Private Issue For The Church Or A Fundamental Issue Of Human Rights?', in *Women-Church*, 12, Autumn, 1993: 18.

165. I. Breward, *History*, 184.

166. Jim McKay and Frank Lewins, 'Religious conflict and integration among some ethnic Christian groups', *Religion in Australia : sociological perspectives*, ed. A.Black, Sydney: Allen & Unwin, 1991, 166-175.

167. James Jupp ed., *The Australian People*, North Ryde: Angus and Robertson, 1988, 939.

168. ibid., 939.

6. Religious culture and the media

169. A. Nichols, *The Communicators: Mass Media and the Australian Church*, Sydney: Pilgrim Publications Limited, 1972, 13.

170. Paul Duffy, *Word of Life in Media and Gospel*, Homebush: St Paul Publications, 1991, cf. also J. Bachman, *Media - Wasteland or Wonderland: Opportunities and Dangers for Christians in the Electronic Age*, Minneapolis: Augsburg Publishing House,1984.

171. Pius XI, 'Qui Arcano', *Actae Apostolicae Sedis* (hereafter ASS), 23 February 1931, 65.

172. Pius XII, *Miranda Prorsus*, Vatican City: Polyglot Press, 1957, 1.

173. ibid., 35.

174. *Inter Mirifica*, Decree on the Means of Social Communication, (December 1963) in A Flannery, ed. *Vatican Council II: The Conciliar and Post Conciliar Documents*, Newtown: E J Dwyer, rev. ed, 1988.

175. Pontifical Commission for the Means of Social Communication, *Pastoral Instruction for the Application of the Decree of the Second Vatican Ecumenical Council on the Means of Social Communication*, London: Catholic Truth Society, 1971.

176. Paul Soukop gives a good coverage of church documents on the media in his article 'Church Documents and the Media', *Concilium: Mass Media*, no 6, 1993, 71-79.

177. G. Bouma, *Religion*, 64.

178. Pius XI, *Vigilanti cura*, AAS, 28, 1936.

179. Pius XII, *Miranda*, 29.

180. P. Soukup, *Church Documents*, 78.

181. G. O'Kelly, 'Switching On', in *Eureka Street*, March 1993, 16-18.

182. ibid., 18.

183. P. Horsfield, 'Larger Than Life: Religious Functions of Television', *Media Information Australia*, 47, February 1988, 61-66.

184. D. Selway, 'Religion in the Print Media', in *Australian Religion Studies Review*, 5, no.2, August 1992, 19.

185. M. Porter, 'The Media and the Women's Ordination Debate', *Australian Religion Studies Review*, 5, no 2, 1992: 12.

186. *SMH*, 19 May 1995, p 1.

187. R. Weston, 'Culture, Music and Aboriginal Media', *Australian Religion Studies Review*, 5, no 2, 1992: 37.

188. I. Breward, *History*, 212.

189. P. Collins, 'The ABC and Religious Broadcasting in Austrlia', in *Australian Religion Studies Review*, 5, no 2, 1992: 17.

190. V. Hinton, 'So What is and What isn't Religious TV?', *Australian Religion Studies Review*, 5, no 2, 1992: 5.

191. P. Collins, *ABC*, 10.

192. ibid., 6.

193. C. McGillion, 'Spirit of Place', *Eureka Street*, 5, no 3, April 1995, 4-5.

194. D. Selway, *Religion*, 20.

195. M. Porter, *Media*, 17.

196. K.Woodward, 'Religion Observed: The Impact of the Medium on the Message', in *Concilium: Mass Media*, no 6, 1993, 99-110.

197. K. Suter, 'Media: The Churches and Peace: from gloom and doom to vision and hope', *Media Information Australia*, no 42, November 1986, 55-59.

198. A. Shboul, 'Islam and the Australian Media: The Implications of Distorting Mirrors', *Australian Religion Studies Review*, 1, no.2, 1988: 23.

199. R. Goutman, 'Anti-Semitism and the Media', *Australian Religion Studies Review*, 1, no 2, 1988: 5-10.

200. A. Nichols, *Communicators*, 27

201. *The Pastoral Instruction*, # 185.

202. P. Horsfield, *Religious Television: The American Experience*, New York: Longman, 1984, for a useful coverage of American religious TV.

203. W. Fore, *Television and Religion: The Shaping of Faith, Values and Culture*, Minneapolis, Augsburg Publishing House, 1987, 98.

204. W. Fore, *Television*, 106-108.

205. P. Horsfield, *Religious*, 11.

206. A. Nichols, *Communicators*, 21.

207. A. Gill, 'God's Radical', in *SMH*, 25 March 1995, p 4A

208. K. Woodward, *Religion Observed*, 108.

209. Pontifical Commission for the Means of Social Communication, *Pastoral Instruction*, # 182.

210. *SMH*, 19 May 1995, p 1.

211. Chris McGillion, 'Good News, bad press', *Eureka Street*, 4, no 3, 1994: 4-5.

212. Brian Gore is an Australian Columban priest noted for his promotion of social justice in the Philippines and in Australia.

213. Chris McGillion, 'Goodbye Mr Chips', *Eureka Street*, 3, no 9, 1993: 4-5.

214. J. Coleman, 'The Sociology of the Media', *Concilium: Mass Media*, no 6, 1993: vii.

215. D. Selway, *Religion*, 23.

216. Mircea Eliade, *Myth and Reality*, quoted by Colin Morris, God-In-A-Box: Christian strategy in the Television Age, London: Hodder and Stoughton, 1983, 171.

217. R. Niebuhr, *Christ and Culture*, New York: Harper, 1951.

218. W. Fore, *Television*, 37.

219. O. Fuchs, 'How the Churches Deal with the Media', *Concilium: Mass Media*, no 6, 1993, 84.

220. J. Metz, 'The Electronic Trap. Theological Remarks on Televised Worship', *Concilium: Mass Media*, no 6, 1993: 59; and J. Coleman, *The Sociology*, 10.

221. M.Russo, 'The Bishops and Abortion: A Case Study in Reporting Church News', in *Concilium: Mass Media*, no 6, 1993, 91-98.

222. P. Bentley, 'Seventh-Day Adventists According to the Sydney Morning Herald', *Australian Religion Studies Review*, 5, no 2, 1992, 32-36.

223. W. Fore, *Television*, 48,49.

224. A. Nichols, *Communicators*, 69.

225. P. Babin, *The New Era in Religious Communication*, Minneapolis: Fortress Press, 1991, 197.

226. *SMH*, 19 May 1995, p 1.

227. W. Fore, *Television*, 116.

Name Index

Subject Index

Bibliography

Advisory Committee on Religious Programmes to the Australian Broadcasting Control Board in conjunction with Australia Frontier, *Religious Telecasting in Australia: An Account of a Consultation held at Ormond College University of Melbourne, August 1966*, Canberra: Advisory Committee on Religious Programmes to the Australian Broadcasting Control Board in conjunction with Australia Frontier, no 1,1968.

Arthur, C. ed, Religion and the Media: *An Introductory Reader*, Cardiff: University of Wales Press, 1993.

Asad, T. *Anthropology and the colonial encounter*, London: Ithaca Press, 1973.

Applebaum, H. ed, *Perspectives in Cultural Anthropology*, New York: State University of New York Press, 1987.

Austin-Broos, D. ed, *Creating Culture: Profiles in the Study of Culture*, Sydney: Allen & Unwin,1987.

Australian Catholic Bishops Conference, *Common Wealth for the Common Good: A Statement on the Distribution of Wealth in Australia*, CollinsDove: North Blackburn, 1992.

Azevedo, M. *Inculturation and the Challenges of Modernity*, Rome: Centre 'Cultures and Religions' - Pontifical Gregorian University, 1982.

Babin, P. *The New Era in Religious Communication*, Minneapolis: Fortress Press, 1991.

Banton, M. *Anthropological approaches to the study of religion*, London: Tavistock, 1966.

Beals, R. et al, *An Introduction to Anthropology*, New York: MacMillan, 5th ed, 1977.

Bentley, P. T. Blombery and P. Hughes, *Faith without Church: Nominalism in Australian Christianity*, Wollstonecraft: Christian Research Association, 1992.

228 • RELIGION IN AUSTRALIAN CULTURE

Berger, P. *The Sacred Canopy*, New York: Anchor, 1969.

Birch, C. *Confronting the Future Australia and the World, the next hundred years*, Ringwood: Penguin, 1976.

Black, A. ed, *Religion in Australia*: Sociological Perspectives, Sydney: Allen & Unwin, 1991.

Bloch, M. *Prey into Hunter*: the politics of religious experience, CUP, 1992.

Blombery, T. and P. Hughes, *Combined Churches Survey for Faith and Mission*, Wollstonecraft: Christian Research Association, 1987.

Blombery, T. *Tomorrow's Church Today: Report for Faith and Mission*, Wollstonecraft: Christian Research Association, 1989.

Blombery, T. *God Through Human Eyes: Report from the Combined Churches Survey*, Wollstonecraft: Christian Research Association, 1989.

Bogle, J. *Caroline Chisholm*, Leominster: Gracewing, 1993.

Bouma, G. *Religion: Meaning, transcendence and community in Australia*, Melbourne: Longman Cheshire, 1992.

Breward, I. Australia - *'The Most Godless Place under Heaven?'*, Melbourne: Beacon Hill Books, 1988.

Breward, I. *A History of the Australian Churches*, St Leonards: Allen & Unwin, 1993.

Brundell, B. 'Australian Secularism and its Challenge', *Compass* 22, no 3 1988: 21-27.

Campion, E. *Rockchoppers: Growing up Catholic in Australia*, Ringwood: Penguin, 1982.

Carrithers, M. *Why humans have cultures*, New York: OUP, 1992.

Coleman, J. and M. Tomka, *Concilium: Mass Media: no 6*, London: SCM Press, 1993.

Collins, P. *God's Earth: Religion as if matter really mattered*, Melbourne: Dove, 1995.

Crombie, G. M. 'Fate and Faith: A Reflection on Australian Culture', *Colloquium* 20, no 1, (1987): 22-30.

Crombie, G.M. 'And God Created Australia', *Interchange* 44 (1988): 13-29.

Dicker, G. 'Kerygma and Australian Culture: The Case of the Aussie Battler', in *Toward Theology in an Australian Context*, ed. V.C. Hayes, Adelaide: AASR, (1979): 46-52.

Dicker, G. 'The Search for Transcendence', *The Shape of Belief*, Sydney: Anzea, 1982: 29-46.

Djiniyini,T. 'Aboriginal Christianity: Based on Indigenous Theology', *Nelen Yubu* 24 (1986): 30-36.

Dobzansky, T. *Mankind Evolving*, New Haven: Yale University Press, 1962.

Dodson, P. 'The Land Our Mother, The Church Our Mother', *Compass* 22, no 1 & 2 (1988): 1-3.

Duncan, B. '40 Years after the s.p.l.i.t.', *National Outlook* 16, no 10, (December 1994): 16-19.

Edwards, D. 'Apprentices in Faith to the Aboriginal View of Land', *Compass* 20, no.1 (1986): 23-29.

Edwards,W. H. 'The Gospel and Aboriginal Culture', *Interchange*, 24 (1978): 195-204.

Engel, F. *Australian Christians in Conflict and Unity 1825-1926*, vol.1, Melbourne: Joint Board of Christian Education, 1984.

Engel, F. *Christians in Australia, Times of Change 1918-1978*, vol. 2, Melbourne: Joint Board of Christian Education, 1993.

Engel, F. *Contemporary Christian Communications: Its Theory and Practice*, New York: Thomas Nelson Publishers, 1975.

Ferguson, G. 'Tears for a Lost Land: the Exilic Experience in Australia', in *The Cultured Pearl*, Melbourne, Victorian Council of Churches, (1986):3-11

Ferguson, G. and Chryssavgis, J. eds, *The Desert is Alive:*

Dimensions of Australian Spirituality, Melbourne: Joint Board of Christian Education, 1990.

Flannery, A. ed, *Vatican Council II*: The Conciliar and Post Conciliar Documents, Newtown: E J Dwyer, rev. ed, 1988;

Fletcher, F. 'Drink from the Well of Oz', *Compass*, 20, no.1 (1986): 16-22.

Flecher, F. 'Culture and Social Theology Within the Australian Context', *Compass*, 22, no 3 (1988): 28-37.

Flecher, F. 'Gospel and Australian Culture', *Compass*, 21, no 1 (1987): 2-6.

Fore, W. *Television and Religion: The Shaping of Faith, Values and Culture*, Minneapolis: Augsburg Publishing House, 1987.

Franzmann, M. & W. Woolnough, 'Interpreting Christ in an Australian Context', *Compass* 20, no 1 (1986): 2-7.

Gardiner, P. *Mary MacKillop*, Newtown: E J Dwyer,1993.

Geertz, C. *The Interpretation of Cultures*, London: Fontana Press, 1973.

Gilchrist, M. *Daniel Mannix: Priest & Patriot*, Blackburn: Dove Communications, 1982.

Gilchrist, M. *Rome or The Bush: The Choice for Australian Catholics*, Melbourne: John XXIII Fellowship Co-op Ltd.,1986.

Goosen, G. 'Boomerang Theology: Reflections on Mateship', *The Australasian Catholic Record*, 64, no.3, (July 1987): 308-314.

Goosen, G. 'A "Boomerang" Environmental Theology' *St Mark's Review* 131, (September 1987): 32-42.

Gondarra, D. 'Father, You Gave Us the Dreaming', *Compass*, 22, no 1 & 2 (1988): 6-8.

Grimshaw, P. et al, *Creating a Nation*, Ringwood: McPheeGribble Publishers,1994.

Harris, D. et al. *The Shape of Belief: Christianity in Australia Today*, Sydney: Lancer,1982.

Haviland, W. *Cultural Anthropology*, New York: Holt, Rinehart and Winston, 6th ed, 1978.

Henderson, G. *Mr Santamaria and the Bishops*, Sydney: St Patrick's College, Manly, 1982.

Hogan, M. *The Sectarian Strand: Religion in Australian History*, Ringwood: Penguin, 1987.

Horne, D. *The Public Culture*, Sydney: Pluto, 1986.

Horsfield, P. *Taming Television: A Parent's Guide to Children and Television*, Sutherland: An Albatross Book, 1986.

Horsfield, P. 'Larger Than Life: Religious Functions of Television', *Media Information Australia*, 47, (February 1988):

Hughes, P. *The Australian Clergy: Report from the Combined Churches Survey*, Wollstonecraft: Christian Research Association,1989.

Hughes, P. *Religion A View from the Australian Census*, Kew: Christian Research Association, 1993.

Hunter, D. and P. Whitten, *The Study of Cultural Anthropology*, New York: Harper and Row, 1976.

Kaldor, P. *Who Goes Where? Who Doesn't Care?* Sydney: Lancer, 1987.

Kaplan, D. and R. Mannes, *Culture Theory*, Englewood Cliffs: Prentice-Hall, 1972.

Luzbetak, L. *The Church and Cultures: an applied anthropology for the religions of the world*, Techny, Illinois: Divine Word Publications, 1970.

Luzbetak, L. *The Church and Cultures: New Perspectives in Missiological Anthropology*, New York: Orbis Books, 1988.

Mackay, H. *Reinventing Australia: The mind and mood of Australia in the 90s*, Sydney: Angus and Robertson, 1993.

Malinowski, B. Magic, *Science and Religion and other essays*, London: Souvenir Press, 1974.

Mayer, H. ed. *Catholics and the Free Society: An Australian Symposium*, Melbourne: F.W. Cheshire, 1961.

McBrien, R. *Catholicism*, Dove Communications: East Malvern, 1983.

McKernan, M. *Australian Churches at War: Attitudes and Activities of the Major Churches 1914-1918*, Sydney: The Catholic Theological Faculty, St Patrick's Manly and Australian War Memorial, 1980.

McLaren, J. 'Radio and Religion', *Media Information Australia*, 41 (August 1986): 41-44.

Molony, J. *History of Australia: The Story of 200 years*, Ringwood: Viking, 1987.

Molony, J. *The Roman Mould of the Australian Catholic Church*, Carlton: Melbourne University Press,1969.

Murphy, R. *Cultural and Social Anthropology: An Overture*, Englewood Cliffs: Prentice Hall,1989.

Nichols, A. *The Communicators: Mass Media and the Australian Church*, Sydney: Pilgrim Productions Limited, 1972.

O'Toole, M. 'Church-Media Relations: A View from the Dog -house', *Doctrine and Life* 41, no 2, (February 1991): 68-74.

Pontifical Commission for the Means of Social Communication, *Pastoral Instruction for the Application of the Decree of the Second Vatican Ecumenical Council on the Means of Social Communication, (Communio et Progressio)* London: Catholic Truth Society, 1971.

Pontifical Council for the Means of Social Communication, *Dawn of a New Era, (Aetatis Novae)*, Boston: St Paul Books and Media, 1992.

Porter, M. *Land of the Spirit?*, Geneva: WCC,1990.

Pius XII, *On Motion Pictures, Radio and Television (Miranda*

Prorsus), Vatican City: Polyglot Press, 1957.

Roseberry, W. *Anthropologies and Histories.: Essays in culture, history and political economy*, New Brunswick: Rutgers University Press, 1991.

Santamaria, B. *Santamaria, Against the Tide*, Melbourne: Oxford University Press, 1981.

Schreiter, R. *Constructing Local Theologies*, New York: Orbis Books, 1986.

Sills, D. ed, 'Marxism', *International Encyclopedia of the Social Sciences*, Vol. 10, New York: Collier-MacMillan, (1972): 46-52.

Stockton, E. *The Aboriginal Gift: Spirituality for a Nation*, Alexandria, Sydney: Millennium Books, 1995.

Swain, T. *Interpreting Aboriginal Religion: An Historical Account*, Bedford Park: Australian Association for the Study of Religions, 1985.

Swain, T. *A Place for Strangers: Towards a history of Australian Aboriginal being*, CUP, 1993.

Thornhill, J. *Making Australia: Exploring our National Conversation*, Sydney: Millennium Books, 1992.

Ungunmerr, M. 'Dadirri', *Compass* 22, no 1 & 2 (1988): 9-11.

Vamplew, ed, *Australians: Historical Statistics*, Sydney: Fairfax, Syme and Weldon Associates, vol.10,1987.

Vatican II Council. *Inter Mirifica, (Decree on the Means of Social Communication)* , in Flannery, A. ed, *Vatican Council II: The Conciliar and Post Conciliar Documents*, Newtown: E J Dwyer, rev. ed, 1988;

Wilson, M. 'Rejoinder: Aboriginal Religion', *Compass* 15, no 1 (1981): 38-40.

Wilson, B. 'Communicating the Gospel in Australia Today', *Interchange* 19, ((1976): 137-148.

Wilson, B. 'Australian Church and Society', *Interchange* 25, (1979): 22-31.

Wilson, B. 'This Christian Country of Ours', *Being Christian in Australia*, (1979): 9-13.

Wilson, B. 'Has God a Future in Industrial Society?', *Interchange* 32 (1983): 20-26.

Wilson, B. 'The Church in a Secular Society' *The Shape of Belief*, ed, D.Harris, Homebush West: Lancer Book, 1983: 1-12.

Wilson, B. *Can God Survive in Australia?* Sydney: Albatross, 1983.

Wilson, B. 'An Aussie Church: 1988 and Beyond', *National Goals and Directions: A Vision for Australia*, Sydney: Albatross, 1987: 31-58.

Wright, D. and E. Clancy, *The Methodists: A History of Methodism in NSW*, Sydney: Allen and Unwin, 1993.